June 5-9, 2017
Urbana-Champaign, IL, USA

I0018428

**Association for
Computing Machinery**

Advancing Computing as a Science & Profession

SIGMETRICS'17

**Abstracts of the 2017 ACM SIGMETRICS / International Conference on
Measurement and Modeling of Computer Systems**

Sponsored by:
ACM SIGMETRICS

Supported by:
Facebook, Google, Huawei, IBM, & Intel

**Association for
Computing Machinery**

Advancing Computing as a Science & Profession

The Association for Computing Machinery
2 Penn Plaza, Suite 701
New York, New York 10121-0701

Notice to Past Authors of ACM-Published Articles
ACM intends to create a complete electronic archive of all articles and/or other material previously published by ACM. If you have written a work that has been previously published by ACM in any journal or conference proceedings prior to 1978, or any SIG Newsletter at any time, and you do NOT want this work to appear in the ACM Digital Library, please inform permissions@acm.org, stating the title of the work, the author(s), and where and when published.

ISBN: 978-1-4503-5032-7 (Digital)

ISBN: 978-1-4503-5593-3 (Print)

Additional copies may be ordered prepaid from:

ACM Order Department
PO Box 30777
New York, NY 10087-0777, USA

Phone: 1-800-342-6626 (USA and Canada)
+1-212-626-0500 (Global)
Fax: +1-212-944-1318
E-mail: acmhelp@acm.org
Hours of Operation: 8:30 am – 4:30 pm ET

Printed in the USA

Message from the General Chairs

Welcome to the 2017 SIGMETRICS Conference on Measurement and Modeling of Computer Systems, held on the campus of the University of Illinois Urbana-Champaign, June 5-9. The conference is the leading research venue in the area of performance analysis of computer systems, and the development of tools and innovative application of tools towards this end.

The conference opens on Monday, June 5, with three workshops: Green Metrics, Workshop on Mathematical Performance Modeling and Analysis (MAMA), and Workshop on Critical Infrastructure Network Security (CINS). The main conference takes place Tuesday – Thursday, June 6-8, with Keynote Talks presented by Michael Jordan and Vahab Mirrokni, lectures from ACM Sigmetrics Achievement Award recipient Sem Borst, ACM Sigmetrics Rising Star Award lecture, 29 regular paper presentations, and roughly 24 poster presentations. The conference wraps up Friday, June 9, with four tutorials by: Nicolas Christin, Jim Dai, Vishal Misra and Richard Ma, and R. Srikant.

SIGMETRICS 2017 was made possible by the hard work of many volunteers, and we would like to thank all of them for their time and dedication. To begin with, the TPC chairs Augustin Chaintreau, Leana Golubchik, and Zhi-Li Zhang assembled a fantastic program committee, and led the review of over 200 papers within a trial dual-deadline submission framework. Their hard work, and the hard work of nearly 60 technical program committee members, selected an outstanding set of papers and posters to be accepted for the conference. Publicity Chairs Ana Bušić and Dah Ming Chiu widely advertised the conference, Workshop Chair Lei Ying arranged an engaging set of workshops, Tutorial Chairs Anshul Gandhi and Vijay Subramanian organized a spectacular set of tutorials, Finance Chair Pramod Viswanath kept us honest, Publications Chair Siddhartha Banerjee ensured a smooth publication process even in the transition to a new journal publication venue, Registration Chair Siva Theja Maguluri carefully configured the registration site, Student Activities Chair Yi Lu arranged for travel support and student oriented activities at the conference, and Webmaster Ashish Khetan kept the website attractive and coherent.

Our secretary, Rachel Palmisano, cheerfully and competently supported local arrangements, and April Mosqus of ACM, skillfully helped smooth conference coordination. We would especially like to thank our industry sponsors, Facebook, Google, Huawei, IBM, and Intel for their generosity and continuing support of SIGMETRICS. Their contributions directly improved the quality and accessibility of the conference.

Enjoy the conference!

Bruce Hajek and Sewoong Oh
SIGMETRICS 2017 General Chairs
University of Illinois at Urbana-Champaign

Message from the Program Chairs

This special issue of Performance Evaluation Review contains extended abstracts of the full papers - appearing in the inaugural issue of the ACM journal, *Proceedings of ACM on Measurement and Analysis of Computing Systems (POMACS)* - and poster papers, all presented at the 2017 ACM SIGMETRICS - the flagship conference of the ACM Special Interest Group for the computer systems performance evaluation community - held in Urbana-Champaign, Illinois, USA, June 5-9, 2017. The conference provides a leading international venue for high-quality research on the development and application of state-of-the-art, broadly applicable analytic, simulation, and measurement-based performance evaluation techniques.

This year's program reflects the sustained ability of the conference to attract high quality submissions while evolving with the broad interests of the performance evaluation community. A wide range of topics – including performance studies of switches, caches, and large-scale systems, vulnerability of networks, efficient storage systems and massive applications, resource allocation and economics, as well as accurate and efficient measurements - are represented in the conference program, showcasing the current developments in performance modeling, analysis, and measurements.

There were 76 papers submitted to the Fall deadline and 127 to the Winter deadline. With a two-round review process, all papers received 3-7 reviews. Nearly all reviews were completed by TPC members, with a limited number provided by external reviewers. Two TPC meetings were held, a virtual one in December and a physical one in March, at Columbia University. As a result of the reviews, online discussions, and TPC meetings, 27 papers and 18 posters appeared in the program. Best paper awards were selected by a small sub-committee of the TPC.

Many people have contributed to the success of ACM SIGMETRICS 2017. Firstly, we would like to thank all the authors for contributing their work. The TPC members were diligent and thorough in their reviews, online discussions, and participation in the TPC meetings. This has also been a transition year, where for the first time, the conference switched to multiple deadlines per year, virtual (in addition to physical) TPC meetings, one-shot (journal-style) revisions, and shepherding of every paper that was accepted by the new ACM POMACS journal and presented at the conference. Consequently, this year's TPC members went above and beyond the (typical) call of duty, and we would like to thank them for their commitment and contributions to the community! Bruce Hajek and **Sewoong** Oh provided much leadership, direction and help on behalf of the organizing committee. Valuable organizational assistance and guidance was also provided by the SIGMETRICS officers, and in particular Vishal Misra and Adam Wierman.

We hope you enjoy SIGMETRICS 2017!

Augustin Chaintreau, Leana Golubchik, and Zhi-Li Zhang
SIGMETRICS 2017 Technical Program Committee co-Chairs

Table of Contents

SIGMETRICS Achievement Award: Sem Borst
Session Chair: Leana Golubchik *(University of Southern California)*

Session 1: Load Balancing among Switch and Caches
Session Chair: Yi Lu *(University of Illinois)*

Session 2: Algorithms for Massive Processing Applications
Session Chair: Y.C. Tay *(National University of Singapore)*

Session 3: Assessing Vulnerability of Large Networks
Session Chair: Adam Wierman *(California Institute of Technology)*

Poster Session

SIGMETRICS Keynote Talk: Vahab Mirrokni

Session Chair: Vishal Misra (*Columbia University*)

Session 4: Performance Analysis of Very Large Systems

Session Chair: Mor Harchol-Balter (*Carnegie Mellon University*)

Session 5: Towards Efficient and Durable Storage

Session Chair: Bhuvan Urgaonkar (*Pennsylvania State University*)

Session 6: New Design for Large Network Applications

Session Chair: Anshul Gandhi (*Stony Brook University*)

SIGMETRICS Keynote Talk: Michael Jordan

Session Chair: Zhi-Li Zhang (*University of Minnesota*)

Session 7: Resource Allocation & Economics
Session Chair: Lei Ying *(Arizona State University)*

SIGMETRICS Rising Star Award: Sewoong Oh
Session Chair: Bruce Hajek *(University of Illinois)*

Session 8: Analyzing and Controlling Network Interaction
Session Chair: Nicolas Gast *(INRIA)*

Session 9: Accurate and Efficient Performance Measurement
Session Chair: Giuliano Casale *(Imperial College)*

Tutorial Session

SIGMETRICS 2017 Conference Organization

General Chairs: Bruce Hajek *(University of Illinois)*
Sewoong Oh *(University of Illinois)*

Program Chairs: Augustin Chaintreau *(Columbia University)*
Leana Golubchik *(University of Southern California)*
Zhi-Li Zhang *(University of Minnesota)*

Publicity Chairs: Ana Bušić *(INRIA and ENS)*
Dah Ming Chui *(The Chinese University of Hong Kong)*

Publications Chair: Siddhartha Banerjee *(Cornell University)*

Workshop Chair: Lei Ying *(Arizona State University)*

Tutorial Chairs: Anshul Gandhi *(Stony Brook University)*
Vijay Subramanian *(University of Michigan)*

Finance Chair: Pramod Viswanath *(University of Illinois)*

Registrations Chair: Siva Thega Maguluri *(Georgia Int. Technology)*

Student Activities Chair: Yi Lu *(University of Illinois)*

Webmaster: Ashsish Khetan *(Univeristy of Illinois)*

Program Committee: Murali Annavaram *(University of Southern California)*
Urtzi Ayesta *(CNRS-LAAS & Ikerbasque-UPV/EHU)*
Thomas Bonald *(Telecom ParisTech)*
Sem Borst *(Bell Labs, Eindhoven University of Technology)*
Niklas Carlsson *(Linkoping University)*
Giuliano Casale *(Imperial College London)*
Augustin Chaintreau *(Columbia University)*
Abhishek Chandra *(University of Minnesota)*
Cheng-Fu Chou *(National Taiwan University)*
Florin Ciucu *(Warwick University)*
Giulia Fanti *(University of Illinois)*
Daniel Figueiredo *(Federal University of Rio de Janeiro)*
Giuliana Franceschinis *(Università del Piemonte Orientale "Amedeo Avogadro")*
Lixin Gao *(University of Massachusetts Amherst)*
Nicolas Gast *(INRIA)*
Javad Ghaderi *(Columbia University)*
Roch Guerin *(Washington University in St. Louis)*
Leana Golubchik *(University of Southern California)*
Mor Harchol-Balter *(Carnegie Mellon University)*

Program Committee (continued):

Nidhi Hegde *(Bell Labs)*
Longbo Huang *(Tsinghua University)*
Sandip Kundu *(University of Massachusetts Amherst)*
Marc Lelarge *(INRIA-ENS)*
Yanhua Li *(Worcester Polytechnic Institute)*
Mingyan Liu *(University of Michigan)*
Yi Lu *(University of Illinois)*
John C.S. Lui *(The Chinese University of Hong Kong)*
Laurent Massoulié *(INRIA, Microsoft Research)*
Michela Meo *(Polytechnic University of Turin)*
Alan Mislove *(Northeastern University)*
Vishal Misra *(Columbia University)*
Eytan Modiano *(Massachusetts Institute of Technology)*
Erich Nahum *(IBM Research)*
Alexandre Proutiere *(KTH Royal Institute of Technology)*
Konstantinos Psounis *(University of Southern California)*
Dan Rubenstein *(Columbia University)*
Shubho Sen *(AT&T Research)*
Stefan Schmid *(Technical University of Berlin)*
Ramesh Sitaraman *(University of Massachusetts Amherst)*
Peter Steenkiste *(Carnegie Mellon University)*
Mark Squillante *(IBM Research)*
Sasha Stolyar *(University of Illinois)*
Y.C. Tay *(National University of Singapore)*
My Thai *(University of Florida)*
Don Towsley *(University of Massachusetts Amherst)*
Bhuvan Urgaonkar *(Pennsylvania State University)*
Steve Uhlig *(Queen Mary University of London)*
Peter Van De Ven *(Centrum Wiskunde & Informatica)*
Benny Van Houdt *(University of Antwerp)*
Milan Vojnovic *(Microsoft Research)*
Anwar Walid *(Nokia Bell-Labs)*
Jia Wang *(AT&T Research)*
Adam Wierman *(California Institute of Technology)*
Carey Williamson *(University of Calgary)*
Cathy Xia *(Ohio State University)*
Cheng-Zhong Xu *(Chinese Academy of Science,*
   Shenzhen Advanced Institute of Technology/Wayne State)
Li Zhang *(IBM Research)*
Zhi-Li Zhang *(University of Minnesota)*
Gil Zussman *(Columbia University)*

SIGMETRICS 2017 Sponsor & Supporters

Sponsor:

Supporters:

Delay Scalings and Mean-Field Limits in Networked Systems

Sem Borst*

Eindhoven University of Technology, 5600 MB Eindhoven, The Netherlands
Nokia Bell Labs, Murray Hill, NJ 07974, USA
sem@win.tue.nl,sem.borst@nokia-bell-labs.com

ABSTRACT

Load balancing mechanisms and scheduling algorithms play a critical role in achieving efficient server utilization and providing robust delay performance in a wide range of networked systems. We will review some celebrated schemes and optimality results which typically assume that detailed state information, e.g. exact knowledge of queue lengths, is available in assigning jobs to queues or allocating a shared resource among competing users. In practice, however, obtaining such state information is non-trivial, and usually involves a significant communication overhead or delay, which is particularly a concern in large-scale networked systems with massive numbers of queues. These scalability issues have prompted increasing attention for the implementation complexity of load balancing and scheduling algorithms as a crucial design criterion, besides the traditional performance metrics.

In this talk we examine the delay performance in such networks for various load balancing and scheduling algorithms, in conjunction with the associated implementation overhead. In the first part of the talk we focus on a scenario with a single dispatcher where jobs arrive that need to be assigned to one of several parallel queues. In the second part of the talk we turn to a system with a single resource, e.g. a shared wireless transmission medium, which is to be allocated among several nodes. We will specifically explore the delay scaling properties in a mean-field framework where the total load and service capacity grow large in proportion. The mean-field regime not only offers analytical tractability, but is also highly relevant given the immense numbers of servers in data centers and cloud networks, and dense populations of wireless devices and sensors in Internet-of-Things (IoT) applications. Time permitting, we will also discuss the impact of the underlying network structure and a few open research challenges.

ACM Reference format:
Sem Borst. 2017. Delay Scalings and Mean-Field Limits in Networked Systems. In *Proceedings of SIGMETRICS '17, June 5–9, 2017, Urbana-Champaign, IL, USA, ,* 1 pages.
DOI: http://dx.doi.org/10.1145/3078505.3080572

---

*Based on joint work with Mark van der Boor, Niek Bouman, Onno Boxma, Fabio Cecchi, Johan van Leeuwaarden, Debankur Mukherjee, Phil Whiting

---

A Low-Complexity Approach to Distributed Cooperative Caching with Geographic Constraints

Konstantin Avrachenkov
INRIA Sophia Antipolis
France
k.avrachenkov@sophia.inria.fr

Jasper Goseling
University of Twente
The Netherlands
j.goseling@utwente.nl

Berksan Serbetci
University of Twente
The Netherlands
b.serbetci@utwente.nl

ABSTRACT

A promising means to increase efficiency of cellular networks compared to existing architectures is to proactively cache data in the base stations. The idea is to store part of the data at the wireless edge and use the backhaul only to refresh the stored data. Data replacement will depend on the users' demand distribution over time. As this distribution is varying slowly, the stored data can be refreshed at off-peak times. In this way, caches containing popular content serve as helpers to the overall system and decrease the maximum backhaul load [1–5].

Our goal in this paper is on developing low-complexity distributed and asynchronous content placement algorithms. This is of practical relevance in cellular networks in which an operator wants to optimize the stored content in caches (i.e., base stations) while keeping the communication in the network to a minimum. In that case it will help that caches exchange information only locally.

We consider continuous and discrete models in which caches are located at arbitrary locations in the plane or in the grid. Caches know their own coverage area as well as the coverage areas of other caches that overlap with this region. There is a content catalog from which users request files according to a known probability distribution. Each cache can store a limited number of files and the goal is to maximize the probability that a user at an arbitrary location in the plane will find the file that she requires in one of the caches that she is covered by. We develop a low-complexity asynchronous distributed cooperative content placement caching algorithms that require communication only between caches with overlapping coverage areas. In the basic algorithm, at each iteration a cache will selfishly update its cache content by minimizing the local miss probability and by considering the content stored by neighbouring caches. We provide a game theoretic perspective on our algorithm and relate the algorithm to the best response dynamics in a potential game. We demonstrate that our algorithm has polynomial step update complexity (in network and catalog size) and has overall convergence in polynomial time. This does not happen in general in potential games. We also provide two simulated annealing-type algorithms (stochastic [6] and deterministic) that finds the best equilibrium corresponding to the global minimum of the miss probability. Finally, we illustrate our results by a number of numerical results with synthetic and real world network models.

To specify, our contributions are as follows:

- We provide a distributed asynchronous algorithm for optimizing the content placement which can be interpreted as giving the best response dynamics in a potential game;
- We prove that the best response dynamics can be obtained as a solution of a convex optimization problem;
- We prove that our algorithm converges and establish polynomial bounds (in terms of network as well as catalog size) on the running time and the complexity per iteration;
- We evaluate our algorithm through numerical examples using a spatial homogeneous Poisson process and base station locations from a real wireless network for the cellular network topology. We demonstrate the hit probability evolution on real and synthetic networks numerically and show that our distributed caching algorithm performs significantly better than storing the most popular content or probabilistic content placement policies or multi-LRU policies. We observe that as the coordination between caches increases, our distributed caching algorithm's performance significantly improves;
- In fact, we demonstrate that in most cases of practical interest the algorithm based on best response converges to the globally optimal content placement;
- Finally, we present simulated annealing type extensions of our algorithm that converge to the globally optimal solution. Our simulated annealing algorithms have efficient practical implementations that we illustrate by numerical examples.

The full paper is available online [7].

KEYWORDS

Caching; Wireless networks; Distributed optimization; Game theory; Simulated annealing

REFERENCES

[1] E. Altman, K. Avrachenkov, and J. Goseling, "Distributed Storage in the Plane", *Networking Conference, IFIP 2014*, pp. 1-9, Trondheim, Norway, June 2014.
[2] E. Bastug, M. Bennis, and M. Debbah, "Cache-enabled Small Cell Networks: Modeling and Tradeoffs", *11th International Symposium on Wireless Communications Systems*, pp. 649-653, 2014.
[3] A. Chattopadhyay, and B. Błaszczyszyn, "Gibbsian On-Line Distributed Content Caching Strategy for Cellular Networks", *arXiv: 1610.02318*, 2016.
[4] A. Giovanidis, and A. Avranas, "Spatial multi-LRU Caching for Wireless Networks with Coverage Overlaps", *ACM SIGMETRICS*, 2016.
[5] N. Golrezaei, A. F. Molisch, A. G. Dimakis, and G. Caire, "Femtocaching and Device-to-Device Collaboration: A New Architecture for Wireless Video Distribution", *IEEE Commun. Mag.*, vol. 51, no. 4, pp. 142-149, April 2013.
[6] B. Hajek, "Cooling schedules for optimal annealing ", *Mathematics of operations research*, vol. 13, no. 2, pp. 311-329, May 1988.
[7] K. Avrachenkov, J. Goseling and B. Serbetci, "A Low-Complexity Approach to Distributed Cooperative Caching with Geographic Constraints", *arXiv: 1704.04465*, 2017.

Optimal Service Elasticity in Large-Scale Distributed Systems*

Debankur Mukherjee
Eindhoven University of Technology
5600 MB, Eindhoven, The Netherlands
d.mukherjee@tue.nl

Souvik Dhara
Eindhoven University of Technology
5600 MB, Eindhoven, The Netherlands
s.dhara@tue.nl

Sem C. Borst[†]
Eindhoven University of Technology
5600 MB, Eindhoven, The Netherlands
s.c.borst@tue.nl

Johan S.H. van Leeuwaarden
Eindhoven University of Technology
5600 MB, Eindhoven, The Netherlands
j.s.h.v.leeuwaarden@tue.nl

ABSTRACT

A fundamental challenge in large-scale cloud networks and data centers is to achieve highly efficient server utilization and limit energy consumption, while providing excellent user-perceived performance in the presence of uncertain and time-varying demand patterns. Auto-scaling provides a popular paradigm for automatically adjusting service capacity in response to demand while meeting performance targets, and queue-driven auto-scaling techniques have been widely investigated in the literature. In typical data center architectures and cloud environments however, no centralized queue is maintained, and load balancing algorithms immediately distribute incoming tasks among parallel queues. In these distributed settings with vast numbers of servers, centralized queue-driven auto-scaling techniques involve a substantial communication overhead and major implementation burden, or may not even be viable at all.

Urged by the above observations, we propose in the present paper a joint auto-scaling and load balancing scheme which does not require any global queue length information or explicit knowledge of system parameters, and yet achieves near-optimal service elasticity. We consider a scenario as described above where arriving tasks must instantaneously be dispatched to one of several parallel servers.

The proposed scheme involves a token-based feedback protocol, allowing the dispatcher to keep track of idle-on servers in standby mode as well as servers in idle-off mode and setup mode. Specifically, when a server becomes idle, it sends a message to the dispatcher to report its status as idle-on. Once a server has remained continuously idle for more than an exponential time with parameter $\mu > 0$ (standby period), it turns off, and sends a message to the dispatcher

to change its status to idle-off. When a task arrives, and there are idle-on servers available, the dispatcher assigns the task to one of them at random, and updates the status of the corresponding server to busy accordingly. Otherwise, the task is assigned to a randomly selected busy server. In the latter event, if there are any idle-off servers, the dispatcher instructs one of them at random to start the setup procedure, and updates the status of the corresponding server from idle-off to setup mode. It then takes an exponential time with parameter $\nu > 0$ (setup period) for the server to become on, at which point it sends a message to the dispatcher to change its status from setup mode to idle-on. Note that a server only sends a (green, say) message when a task completion leaves its queue empty, and sends at most one (red, say) message when it turns off after a standby period per green message, so that at most two messages are generated per task.

In order to analyze the response time performance and energy consumption of the proposed scheme, we consider a scenario with N homogeneous servers, and establish the fluid-level dynamics for the proposed scheme in a regime where the total task arrival rate and nominal number of servers grow large in proportion. This regime not only offers analytical tractability, but is also highly relevant given the massive numbers of servers in data centers and cloud networks. The fluid-limit results show that the proposed scheme achieves asymptotic optimality in terms of response time performance as well as energy consumption. Specifically, we prove that for any positive values of μ and ν both the waiting time incurred by tasks and the relative energy portion consumed by idle servers vanish in the limit. To the best of our knowledge, this is the first scheme to provide auto-scaling capabilities in a setting with distributed queues and achieve near-optimal service elasticity. Extensive simulation experiments corroborate the fluid-limit results, and demonstrate that the proposed scheme can match the user performance and energy consumption of state-of-the-art approaches that do assume the full benefit of a centralized queue.

* Formal statements, numerical experiments, and the rigorous proofs can be found in the full version: https://arxiv.org/abs/1703.08373

† Also with Nokia Bell Labs, Murray Hill, NJ, USA.

ACM Reference format:
Debankur Mukherjee, Souvik Dhara, Sem C. Borst, and Johan S.H. van Leeuwaarden. 2017. Optimal Service Elasticity in Large-Scale Distributed Systems. In *Proceedings of SIGMETRICS '17, June 5–9, 2017, Urbana-Champaign, IL, USA,* , 1 pages.
DOI: http://dx.doi.org/10.1145/3078505.3078532

Queue-Proportional Sampling: A Better Approach to Crossbar Scheduling for Input-Queued Switches[*]

Long Gong
Georgia Institute of Technology
gonglong@gatech.edu

Paul Tune
University of Adelaide
School of Mathematical Sciences
paul.tune@adelaide.edu.au

Liang Liu
Georgia Institute of Technology
lliu315@gatech.edu

Sen Yang
Georgia Institute of Technology
sen.yang@gatech.edu

Jun (Jim) Xu
Georgia Institute of Technology
jx@cc.gatech.edu

ABSTRACT

Most present day switching systems, in Internet routers and data-center switches, employ a single input-queued crossbar to interconnect input ports with output ports. Such switches need to compute a matching, between input and output ports, for each switching cycle (time slot). The main challenge in designing such matching algorithms is to deal with the unfortunate tradeoff between the quality of the computed matching and the computational complexity of the algorithm. In this paper, we propose a general approach that can significantly boost the performance of both SERENA and iSLIP, yet incurs only $O(1)$ additional computational complexity at each input/output port. Our approach is a novel proposing strategy, called *Queue-Proportional Sampling (QPS)*, that generates an excellent *starter matching*. We show, through rigorous simulations, that when starting with this starter matching, iSLIP and SERENA can output much better final matching decisions, as measured by the resulting throughput and delay performance, than they otherwise can.

CCS CONCEPTS

• **Mathematics of computing** → *Matchings and factors*; *Queueing theory*; • **Theory of computation** → *Scheduling algorithms*; • **Networks** → *Network resources allocation*;

KEYWORDS

Crossbar scheduling; input-queued switch; queue-proportional sampling; matching

ACM Reference format:
Long Gong, Paul Tune, Liang Liu, Sen Yang, and Jun (Jim) Xu. 2017. Queue-Proportional Sampling: A Better Approach to Crossbar Scheduling for Input-Queued Switches. In *Proceedings of SIGMETRICS '17, Urbana-Champaign, IL, USA, June 5–9, 2017,* 1 pages.
DOI: http://dx.doi.org/10.1145/3078505.3078509

ACKNOWLEDGMENTS

We thank Prof. Bill Lin for sharing with us the simulation code for iSLIP and SERENA. This work is supported in part by US NSF grants CNS-1423182, CNS-1302197 and, Australian Research Council grant DP110103505.

---

[*]The full version of this paper is available at https://goo.gl/R3Q5U7.

Hieroglyph: Locally-Sufficient Graph Processing via Compute-Sync-Merge

Xiaoen Ju
University of Michigan
jux@umich.edu

Hani Jamjoom
IBM T.J. Watson Research Center
jamjoom@us.ibm.com

Kang G. Shin
University of Michigan
kgshin@umich.edu

ACM Reference format:
Xiaoen Ju, Hani Jamjoom, and Kang G. Shin. 2017. Hieroglyph: Locally-Sufficient Graph Processing via Compute-Sync-Merge. In *Proceedings of SIGMETRICS '17, June 5–9, 2017, Urbana-Champaign, IL, USA, ,* 1 pages.
DOI: http://dx.doi.org/10.1145/3078505.3078589

Mainstream graph processing systems (such as Pregel [3] and PowerGraph [1]) follow the bulk synchronous parallel model. This design leads to the tight coupling of computation and communication, where no vertex can proceed to the next iteration of computation until all vertices have been processed in the current iteration and graph states have been synchronized across all hosts. This coupling of computation and communication incurs significant performance penalty.

Fully decoupling computation from communication requires (*i*) restricted access to only local state during computation and (*ii*) independence of inter-host communication from computation. We call the combination of both conditions *local sufficiency*. Local sufficiency is not efficiently supported by state of the art. Synchronous systems, by design, do not support local sufficiency due to their intrinsic computation-communication coupling. Even systems that implement asynchronous execution only partially achieve local sufficiency. For example, PowerGraph's asynchronous mode satisfies local sufficiency by distributed scheduling. If a vertex-centric function uses remote state, then it will not be marked as ready for execution until its remote input becomes locally available. Thus, the function itself is not locally sufficient. GiraphUC [2] avoids such a cost by concentrating computation on master vertex replicas, efficiently supporting local sufficiency for edge-cut partitioning. But this approach does not support vertex-cut and thus cannot benefit from its balanced workload distribution.

Towards efficient support for local sufficiency, we set two design goals. The first goal is to activate vertex-centric computation on all vertex replicas, enabling each replica to independently update its state. This relaxed consistency model would support vertex-cut and enable fast local state propagation without inter-host coordination. The second goal is to enforce local sufficiency at the programming abstraction level. This would eliminate any related coordination overhead at the system level. Additionally, any inconsistency would be resolved by user-defined functions, which are coordinated across all hosts to achieve global consistency upon convergence.

Following these design choices, we introduce a new programming abstraction called *Compute-Sync-Merge* (CSM). *Compute* defines locally-sufficient vertex-centric computation, which has access only to local input state. *Sync* and *Merge* coordinate the execution on all hosts. The former is in charge of state propagation and the latter is responsible for the merging of remote updates with local state. Together, they resolve the inconsistency caused by locally-sufficient computation.

We demonstrate the expressiveness and simplicity of CSM by implementing several widely-used single-phase algorithms, such as PageRank, single-source shortest path, and weakly connected component. The CSM abstraction also provides a new dimension for designing efficient locally-sufficient multi-phase graph algorithms. In general, multi-phase algorithms limit the performance gains of locally-sufficient computation due to global synchronization at phase boundaries [2]. CSM, however, enables the design of multi-phase algorithms in which (*i*) locally-sufficient computation freely proceeds beyond phase boundaries and (*ii*) conflicting state due to computation with local input is resolved in *Sync* and *Merge*. We exemplify such use of CSM with an efficient new design of a multi-phase maximal bipartite matching algorithm.

We have fully implemented *Hieroglyph*, a graph processing system supporting CSM. Experiments with real-world graphs show that Hieroglyph outperforms state of the art by up to 53x, with a median speedup of 3.5x and an average speedup of 6x.[1]

Acknowledgments. We thank the anonymous reviewers and our shepherd, Abhishek Chandra, for their feedback. The work reported in this paper was supported in part by Intel Corporation.

REFERENCES
[1] Joseph E. Gonzalez, Yucheng Low, Haijie Gu, Danny Bickson, and Carlos Guestrin. PowerGraph: Distributed Graph-parallel Computation on Natural Graphs. In *OSDI'12*.
[2] Minyang Han and Khuzaima Daudjee. 2015. Giraph Unchained: Barrierless Asynchronous Parallel Execution in Pregel-like Graph Processing Systems. *Proc. VLDB Endow.* 8, 9 (May 2015).
[3] Grzegorz Malewicz, Matthew H. Austern, Aart J.C Bik, James C. Dehnert, Ilan Horn, Naty Leiser, and Grzegorz Czajkowski. Pregel: A System for Large-scale Graph Processing. In *SIGMOD'10*.

[1] The full version of this paper is available kabru.eecs.umich.edu.

A Simple Yet Effective Balanced Edge Partition Model for Parallel Computing

Lingda Li*
Brookhaven National Laboratory
lli@bnl.gov

Robel Geda
Rutgers University
rag152@scarletmail.rutgers.edu

Ari B. Hayes
Rutgers University
arihayes@cs.rutgers.edu

Yanhao Chen
Rutgers University
yc827@scarletmail.rutgers.edu

Pranav Chaudhari
Rutgers University
pc602@scarletmail.rutgers.edu

Eddy Z. Zhang
Rutgers University
eddy.zhengzhang@cs.rutgers.edu

Mario Szegedy
Rutgers University
szegedy@cs.rutgers.edu

ABSTRACT

Graph edge partition models have recently become an appealing alternative to graph vertex partition models for distributed computing due to both their flexibility in balancing loads and their performance in reducing communication cost.

In this paper, we propose a simple yet effective graph edge partitioning algorithm. In practice, our algorithm provides good partition quality while maintaining low partition overhead. It also outperforms similar state-of-the-art edge partition approaches, especially for power-law graphs. In theory, previous work showed that an approximation guarantee of $O(d_{max}\sqrt{\log n \log k})$ apply to the graphs with $m = \Omega(k^2)$ edges (n is the number of vertices, and k is the number of partitions). We further rigorously proved that this approximation guarantee hold for all graphs.

We also demonstrate the applicability of the proposed edge partition algorithm in real parallel computing systems. We draw our example from GPU program locality enhancement and demonstrate that the graph edge partition model does not only apply to distributed computing with many computer nodes, but also to parallel computing in a single computer node with a many-core processor.

CCS CONCEPTS

•**Mathematics of computing** → **Graph algorithms;** •**Theory of computation** → **Parallel computing models;** •**Computing methodologies** → *Modeling and simulation;*

KEYWORDS

Graph model; edge partition; GPU; data sharing; program locality

ACM Reference format:
Lingda Li, Robel Geda, Ari B. Hayes, Yanhao Chen, Pranav Chaudhari, Eddy Z. Zhang, and Mario Szegedy. 2017. A Simple Yet Effective Balanced Edge Partition Model for Parallel Computing. In *Proceedings of SIGMETRICS '17, June 5–9, 2017, Urbana-Champaign, IL, USA, , 1 pages.*
DOI: http://dx.doi.org/10.1145/3078505.3078520

The full paper is available at https://www.cs.rutgers.edu/~zz124/sigmetrics17.pdf.

---

*This work was done when Lingda Li was a Postdoctoral Associate at Rutgers University.

SIGMETRICS '17, June 5–9, 2017, Urbana-Champaign, IL, USA
© 2017 Copyright held by the owner/author(s). ACM ISBN 978-1-4503-5032-7/17/06.
DOI: http://dx.doi.org/10.1145/3078505.3078520

Overcommitment in Cloud Services
Bin packing with Chance Constraints

Maxime C. Cohen
New York University (NYU) - Leonard N. Stern School of
Business

Philipp Keller
Google, Inc.

Vahab Mirrokni
Google, Inc.

Morteza Zadimoghaddam
Google, Inc.

ABSTRACT

This paper considers a traditional problem of resource allocation, scheduling jobs on machines. One such recent application is cloud computing, where jobs arrive in an online fashion with capacity requirements and need to be immediately scheduled on physical machines in data centers. It is often observed that the requested capacities are not fully utilized, hence offering an opportunity to employ an *overcommitment policy*, i.e., selling resources beyond capacity. Setting the right overcommitment level can induce a significant cost reduction for the cloud provider, while only inducing a very low risk of violating capacity constraints. We introduce and study a model that quantifies the value of overcommitment by modeling the problem as a bin packing with chance constraints. We then propose an alternative formulation that transforms each chance constraint into a submodular function. We show that our model captures the risk pooling effect and can guide scheduling and overcommitment decisions. We also develop a family of online algorithms that are intuitive, easy to implement and provide a constant factor guarantee from optimal. Finally, we calibrate our model using realistic workload data, and test our approach in a practical setting. Our analysis and experiments illustrate the benefit of overcommitment in cloud services, and suggest a cost reduction of 1.5% to 17% depending on the provider's risk tolerance.

ACM Reference format:
Maxime C. Cohen, Philipp Keller, Vahab Mirrokni, and Morteza Zadimoghaddam. 2017. Overcommitment in Cloud Services
Bin packing with Chance Constraints. In *Proceedings of SIGMETRICS '17, June 5-9, 2017, Urbana-Champaign, IL, USA, , 1 pages.*
DOI: http://dx.doi.org/10.1145/3078505.3078530

*The full version of this paper is available at https://papers.ssrn.com

Investigation of the 2016 Linux TCP Stack Vulnerability at Scale

Alan Quach[*]
University of California, Riverside
aquac005@ucr.edu

Zhongjie Wang[*]
University of California, Riverside
zwang048@ucr.edu

Zhiyun Qian
University of California, Riverside
zhiyunq@cs.ucr.edu

1 INTRODUCTION

To combat blind in-window attacks against TCP, changes proposed in RFC 5961 have been implemented by Linux since late 2012. While successfully eliminating the old vulnerabilities, the new TCP implementation was reported in August 2016 to have introduced a subtle yet serious security flaw [1]. Assigned CVE-2016-5696, the flaw exploits the challenge ACK rate limiting feature that could allow an off-path attacker to infer the presence/absence of a TCP connection between two arbitrary hosts, terminate such a connection, and even inject malicious payload. In this work, we perform a comprehensive measurement of the impact of the new vulnerability. This includes (1) tracking the vulnerable Internet servers, (2) monitoring the patch behavior over time, (3) picturing the overall security status of TCP stacks at scale. Towards this goal, we design a scalable measurement methodology to scan the Alexa top 1 million websites for almost 6 months. We also present how notifications impact the patching behavior, and compare the result with the Heartbleed [2] and the Debian PRNG vulnerability [4]. The measurement represents a valuable data point in understanding how Internet servers react to serious security flaws in the operating system kernel.

2 METHODOLOGY

Our basic approach is to initiate a regular TCP connection with a server and identify its vulnerability by sending a series of probing packets. Corresponding to 3 types of challenge ACKs (SYN/ACK/RST), our scan is comprised of 3 major tests, and each test sends 210 corresponding probing packets in 1/3 second to fully exhaust the server's challenge ACK rate limit counter. The whole scan is stateful and consists of multiple stages. We use a decision tree to guide our scan and to classify the server into vulnerable, version-1 patched, version-2 patched, non-RFC5961-compliant and firewall cases.

To cope with large-scale scans, we designed a highly efficient parallel scanning methodology, inspired by ZMap [3]. We use fine-grained timing control inside a single sending thread to enforce the strong timing requirement of our scan. Due to the necessary fixed-length intervals between rounds and subscans, we multiplex the idle time by scheduling other batches of target IPs. With this packet scheduling scheme, we can maximize the network utilization and have a full control of scanning speed and packet loss rate.

[*]Both authors contributed equally.

[†]The full paper of this work may be found at http://www.cs.ucr.edu/~zhiyunq/pub/sigmetrics17_cack_measurement.pdf

3 RESULT

We started our scans of Alexa's top 10,000 sites 9 days after the public disclosure of the vulnerability, and top 1 million sites 20 days later, and continued them for almost 6 months.

We estimate about 67% of the Alexa's top 10,000 sites were initially vulnerable. 9 days after the vulnerability went fully public, 33% of the IPs for the Alexa's top 100 websites and 26% of the top 10,000 websites were vulnerable. The numbers gradually dropped to below 10% and 15% respectively at the end, showing a "long tail". Interestingly, compared to top 1K and 1M websites, a larger fraction of Top 100 websites were initially vulnerable but eventually they caught up. We hypothesize that due to stability requirements the top sites are likely choosing a longer patching period.

Another important factor is the delegation of security management of a server. We find that managed hostings including CDNs have diverse patching behaviors. While some CDN providers (e.g., CloudFlare) have a perfect 100% patch rate from the first day of our measurement, some other providers (e.g., Amazon CloudFront) never patched their servers even 6 months after disclosure. Meanwhile, unmanaged hostings show an overall slower patch process.

In addition to our measurement, we send notifications to vulnerable websites. The result showed the patch rate doubled for these websites compared to the control group after 3 weeks.

4 CONCLUSION

In this work we analyzed the impact of the recent challenge ACK vulnerability in Linux kernel, including (1) who was initially vulnerable, (2) patching behavior over time, by hosting services, and by network services (3) how notification affects the patching behavior. In general, we find that many in the top websites were vulnerable and remain vulnerable for an extended period of time. We find that the hosting services behind many of the top websites in fact have a surprisingly diverse and sometimes opposite patching behavior. We show that Linux kernel patching has some interesting differences from the recent Heartbleed and the Debian weak key event. The lessons and data collected will hopefully help the community better react to future Internet-wide security events.

REFERENCES

[1] Yue Cao, Zhiyun Qian, Zhongjie Wang, Tuan Dao, Srikanth V. Krishnamurthy, and Lisa M. Marvel. 2016. Off-Path TCP Exploits: Global Rate Limit Considered Dangerous. In *25th USENIX Security Symposium (USENIX Security 16)*.
[2] Zakir Durumeric, James Kasten, David Adrian, J. Alex Halderman, Michael Bailey, Frank Li, Nicolas Weaver, Johanna Amann, Jethro Beekman, Mathias Payer, and Vern Paxson. 2014. The Matter of Heartbleed. In *Proceedings of the 2014 Conference on Internet Measurement Conference (IMC '14)*.
[3] Zakir Durumeric, Eric Wustrow, and J. Alex Halderman. 2013. ZMap: Fast Internet-wide Scanning and Its Security Applications. In *Presented as part of the 22nd USENIX Security Symposium (USENIX Security 13)*.
[4] Scott Yilek, Eric Rescorla, Hovav Shacham, Brandon Enright, and Stefan Savage. 2009. When Private Keys Are Public: Results from the 2008 Debian OpenSSL Vulnerability. In *Proceedings of the 9th ACM SIGCOMM Conference on Internet Measurement Conference (IMC '09)*.

Characterizing and Modeling Patching Practices of Industrial Control Systems*

Brandon Wang
The University of Iowa, USA

Xiaoye Li
The University of Iowa, USA

Leandro P. de Aguiar
Siemens Corporation, USA

Daniel S. Menasche
Federal University of Rio de Janeiro
(UFRJ), Brazil

Zubair Shafiq
The University of Iowa, USA

ABSTRACT

Industrial Control Systems (ICS) are widely deployed in mission critical infrastructures such as manufacturing, energy, and transportation. The mission critical nature of ICS devices poses important security challenges for ICS vendors and asset owners. In particular, the patching of ICS devices is usually deferred to scheduled production outages so as to prevent potential operational disruption of critical systems. In this paper, we present the results from our longitudinal measurement and characterization study of ICS patching behavior. Our analysis of more than 100 thousand Internet-exposed ICS devices reveals that fewer than 30% upgrade to newer patched versions within 60 days of a vulnerability disclosure. Based on our measurement and analysis, we further propose a model to forecast the patching behavior of ICS devices.

CCS CONCEPTS

• **Security and privacy** → **Network security**; • **Networks** → *Network measurement*;

KEYWORDS

Industrial Control Systems (ICS); Shodan; Vulnerability Patching

ACM Reference format:
Brandon Wang, Xiaoye Li, Leandro P. de Aguiar, Daniel S. Menasche, and Zubair Shafiq. 2017. Characterizing and Modeling Patching Practices of Industrial Control Systems. In *Proceedings of SIGMETRICS '17, June 5–9, 2017, Urbana-Champaign, IL, USA,* , 1 pages.
DOI: http://dx.doi.org/10.1145/3078505.3078524

1 INTRODUCTION

Background and Motivation. Industrial Control Systems (ICS) are increasingly being used for a wide range of applications such as industrial automation, utility monitoring, and asset tracking [1, 4]. As any piece of software, ICS products are subject to bugs and vulnerabilities. However, unlike ordinary systems, ICS devices pose a unique set of challenges. Bugs and vulnerabilities in ICS software

---

*The full version of the paper is available at http://cs.uiowa.edu/~mshafiq/files/wang-sigmetrics2017.pdf.

modules can cause serious consequences but frequent patching of such systems may lead to intolerable unavailability of mission critical infrastructures. Although there have been a number of reports indicating that ICS patching behavior is erratic [2], such reports are typically conducted under restrictive non-disclosure agreements. Our goal, in contrast, is to analyze the ICS ecosystem using a reproducible methodology and publicly available data.

Key Findings. We summarize our proposed approach and key findings as follows.

First, we conduct a longitudinal measurement study to systematically analyze ICS patching behavior. We analyze 3 years worth of IPv4 scanning data from Shodan [3] for more than 500 known ICS protocols and products. We conduct a longitudinal study to analyze the impact of vulnerability disclosures on ICS device patching. *Our key insight consists of cross correlating the reports provided by Shodan with public data available in other sites such as the National Vulnerability Database (NVD) and the websites of ICS device vendors.* By jointly analyzing these data, we are able not only to assess whether the disclosure of vulnerabilities is correlated with patch application, but also if and when different features associated to the disclosed vulnerabilities, such as their Common Vulnerability Scoring System (CVSS) scores, impact patching behavior. Our analysis of more than 100 thousand ICS devices reveals that less than 30% of products exhibit average version increases within 60 days of vulnerability disclosure.

Second, we propose a variation of the Bass model to capture and forecast the dynamics of ICS population and patching behavior. Our results show that the Bass model provides comparable accuracy as traditional ARIMA based time series prediction models, while requiring less parameters whose meaning is amenable to direct physical interpretation. Our population forecasting models can be helpful for asset owners and vendors to inform strategic patch management policies for ICS devices.

Acknowledgments. We would like to thank John Matherly for providing us free access to the Shodan database. We would also like to thank our shepherd, Gil Zussman, and the anonymous reviewers for their valuable feedback.

REFERENCES

[1] Xuan Feng, Qiang Li, Haining Wang, and Limin Sun. 2016. Characterizing industrial control system devices on the Internet. In *IEEE ICNP*.
[2] Wolfgang Kandek. 2009. The laws of vulnerabilities 2.0. (2009). BlackHat, Las Vegas, NV, USA.
[3] John Matherly. 2017. Shodan. https://www.shodan.io. (2017).
[4] Ariana Mirian, Zane Ma, David Adrian, Matthew Tischer, Thasphon Chuenchujit, Tim Yardley, Robin Berthier, Joshua Mason, Zakir Durumeric, J Alex Halderman, and others. 2016. An Internet-Wide View of ICS Devices. In *IEEE PST*.

Security Game with Non-additive Utilities and Multiple Attacker Resources

Sinong Wang
The Ohio State University
2015 Neil Avenue
Columbus, Ohio 43210
wang.7691@osu.edu

Ness Shroff
The Ohio State University
2015 Neil Avenue
Columbus, Ohio 43210
shroff.11@osu.edu

ABSTRACT

There has been significant interest in studying security games for modeling the interplay of attacks and defenses on various systems involving critical infrastructure, financial system security, political campaigns, and civil safeguarding. However, existing security game models typically either assume additive utility functions, or that the attacker can attack only one target. Such assumptions lead to tractable analysis, but miss key inherent dependencies that exist among different targets in current complex networks. In this paper, we generalize the classical security game models to allow for non-additive utility functions. We also allow attackers to be able to attack multiple targets. We examine such a general security game from a theoretical perspective and provide a unified view. In particular, we show that each security game is equivalent to a combinatorial optimization problem over a set system ε, which consists of defender's pure strategy space. The key technique we use is based on the transformation, projection of a polytope, and the ellipsoid method. This work settles several open questions in security game domain and extends the state-of-the-art of both the polynomial solvable and NP-hard class of the security game.

KEYWORDS

Security games; computational game theory; complexity

ACM Reference format:
Sinong Wang and Ness Shroff. 2017. Security Game with Non-additive Utilities and Multiple Attacker Resources. In *Proceedings of SIGMETRICS '17, Urbana-Champaign, IL, USA, June 05-09, 2017*, 1 pages.
https://doi.org/http://dx.doi.org/10.1145/3078505.3078519

1 INTRODUCTION

In this paper, we study the classic *security game* model [2] when attacker has multiple resources and utility functions are non-additive. More specifically, we wonder how the following questions that are well understood in the case of single attacker resource and additive utility functions can be addressed in this general case: (1) how to compactly represent the security game with multiple attacker resources and the non-additive utility functions? (2) how to efficiently solve such a compactly represented game? (3) what is the

complexity of the security game when we consider non-additive utility functions and allow the attackers to attack multiple attacker resources?

2 MAIN RESULTS

To answer these questions, we provide the following contributions: (1) we first propose a polytope transformation and projection framework to equivalently and compactly represent the zero-sum and non-additive security game with only poly(n) variables; (2) We prove that the problem of determining the Nash equilibrium of the zero-sum and non-additive security game and the problem of optimizing a *Pseudo Boolean* function over a set system ε can be reduced to each other in polynomial time. (3) We then apply our framework to the non-zero-sum and non-additive security game, and further obtain a similar result that determining the strong Stackelberg equilibrium and the above combinatorial optimization problem is equivalent. (4) Finally, we examine the Nash equilibrium in the non-zero-sum but additive security game. We prove that determining the Nash equilibrium can be reduced to the linear optimization over a set system ε.

3 CONCLUSIONS

These results demonstrate that the security game with non-additive utility function and multiple attacker resource is essentially a combinatorial problem, and provide a systematic framework to transform the game-theoretical problem to the problem of combinatorial algorithm design. Further, our results not only answers the questions proposed in the security game domain [1, 4], but also extends significantly both the polynomial solvable and NP-hard class. The full version of the paper is available at [3].

4 ACKNOWLEDGMENTS

This work has been supported in part by a grant from the Army Research Office W911NF-15-1-0277, a grant from the Defense Thrust Reduction Agency HDTRA1-14-1-0058, and a grant from the the Office of Naval Research N00014-15-1-2166.

REFERENCES

[1] Dmytro Korzhyk, Vincent Conitzer, and Ronald Parr. 2011. Security games with multiple attacker resources. In *IJCAI Proceedings-International Joint Conference on Artificial Intelligence*, Vol. 22. Citeseer, 273–279.
[2] M. Tambe. 2011. *Security and game theory: Algorithms, deployed systems, lessons learned.* Cambridge University Press.
[3] Sinong Wang and Ness Shroff. 2017. Security Game with Non-additive Utilities and Multiple Attacker Resources. *https://arxiv.org/pdf/1701.08644.pdf* (2017).
[4] Haifeng Xu. 2016. The mysteries of security games: Equilibrium computation becomes combinatorial algorithm design. In *Proceedings of the 2016 ACM Conference on Economics and Computation*. ACM, 497–514.

Fluid-Model-Based Car Routing for Modern Ridesharing Systems

Anton Braverman
Cornell University
ab2329@cornell.edu

J.G. Dai
Cornell University
jim.dai@cornell.edu

Xin Liu
Arizona State University
xliu272@asu.edu

Lei Ying
Arizona State University
lei.ying.2@asu.edu

ABSTRACT

This paper considers a closed queueing network model of ridesharing systems such as Didi Chuxing, Lyft, and Uber. We focus on empty-car routing, a mechanism by which we control car flow in the network to optimize system-wide utility functions, e.g. the availability of empty cars when a passenger arrives. We establish both process-level and steady-state convergence of the queueing network to a fluid limit in a large market regime where demand for rides and supply of cars tend to infinity, and use this limit to study a fluid-based optimization problem. We prove that the optimal network utility obtained from the fluid-based optimization is an upper bound on the utility in the finite car system for any routing policy, both static and dynamic, under which the closed queueing network has a stationary distribution. This upper bound is achieved asymptotically under the fluid-based optimal routing policy. Simulation results with real-word data released by Didi Chuxing demonstrate that the utility under the fluid-based optimal routing policy converges to the upper bound with a rate of $1/\sqrt{N}$.

1 INTRODUCTION

Because of the proliferation of ridesharing services, modeling and control of these systems have become important research topics over the last few years. This work focuses on empty-car routing mechanisms for controlling car flows in the network to optimize system-wide utility functions [2].

We consider a system with $r > 0$ regions and $N > 0$ cars. The regions can be interpreted as geographic regions in a city and cars drive around between regions transporting passengers. At time $t = 0$, all cars start off idling empty in some region, waiting for a passenger. Passengers arrive to region i according to a Poisson process with rate $N\lambda_i > 0$, and arrivals to different regions are independent. When a passenger arrives to region i, if there is an empty car available there, then the passenger occupies that car and travels to region j with probability P_{ij}. We allow $P_{ii} > 0$ to represent trips within a region. Travel times from region i to j have mean $1/\mu_{ij}$ and are assumed to be i.i.d. exponential random

SIGMETRICS '17, June 5–9, 2017, Urbana-Champaign, IL, USA
© 2017 Copyright held by the owner/author(s). ACM ISBN 978-1-4503-5032-7/17/06.
DOI: http://dx.doi.org/10.1145/3078505.3078595

variables, although our main results hold without this assumption. If no empty car is available, the passenger abandons the system and finds an alternative form of transportation to the destination. Once the passenger arrives at region j, the car becomes empty. The empty car can either decide to stay in region j (and wait for a new passenger) with probability Q_{jj}, or drive empty to a different region k and wait for a passenger there with probability Q_{jk}. In general, the routing matrix (also called the routing policy) $Q = (Q_{ij})$ is allowed to be *state-dependent*, i.e. Q may depend on the current distribution of cars in the system. We assume N, λ, μ, and $P = (P_{ij})$ are given, and seek to choose Q to optimize a system-wide utility function, e.g., to maximize system-wide availability of empty cars. To model these dynamics, we use a closed queueing network that belongs to the class of BCMP networks [1].

2 THE RIDESHARING OPTIMIZATION PROBLEM

In this section we introduce the fluid-based optimization and state our main results, Theorems 2.1 and 2.2. Let $E_{ij}^{(N)}(t)$ and $F_{ij}^{(N)}(t)$ be the number of empty and full cars en route from region i to region, respectively, where $E_{ii}^{(N)}(t)$ is interpreted the number of empty cars waiting in region i for a new passenger. Furthermore, define $\tilde{E}_{ij}^{(N)}(t) = \frac{1}{N}E_{ij}^{(N)}(t)$, $\tilde{F}_{ij}^{(N)}(t) = \frac{1}{N}F_{ij}^{(N)}(t)$ and $A_i^{(N)} = \mathbb{P}(\tilde{E}_{ii}^{(N)}(\infty) > 0)$ to be the availability at region i. Let $\tilde{E}^{(N)}(t)$, $\tilde{F}^{(N)}(t)$ and $A^{(N)}$ be their corresponding matrix and vector versions.

We now consider the fluid-based optimization problem to be fully specified from (1) to (8) below. In the optimization problem, $c_i > 0$ are rewards for picking up a passenger at region i, and $\tilde{c}_{ij} > 0$ are costs of sending empty cars from i to j. The variables in the optimization problem are q, $\bar{e}$, $\bar{f}$, $\bar{a}$. Let $q = (q_{ij})$ be an $r \times r$ matrix representing a static empty-car routing policy Q. Let $\bar{e}$, $\bar{f}$, and $\bar{a}$ represent $\mathbb{E}[\tilde{E}^{(N)}(\infty)]$, $\mathbb{E}[\tilde{F}^{(N)}(\infty)]$ and $A^{(N)}$ in the ridesharing network, respectively.

$$\max_{q, \bar{e}, \bar{f}, \bar{a}} \sum_{i=1}^{r} c_i \lambda_i \bar{a}_i - \sum_{i=1}^{r} \sum_{j=1, j\neq i}^{r} \tilde{c}_{ij} \bar{e}_{ij} \quad (1)$$

$$\text{subject to} \quad \lambda_i P_{ij} \bar{a}_i = \mu_{ij} \bar{f}_{ij}, \quad (2)$$

$$\mu_{ij} \bar{e}_{ij} = q_{ij} \sum_{k=1}^{r} \mu_{ki} \bar{f}_{ki}, \quad (3)$$

$$\lambda_i \bar{a}_i = \sum_{k=1, k \neq i}^{r} \mu_{ki} \bar{e}_{ki} + q_{ii} \sum_{k=1}^{r} \mu_{ki} \bar{f}_{ki}, \quad (4)$$

$$(1 - \bar{a}_i)\bar{e}_{ii} = 0, \quad (5)$$

$$\sum_{i=1}^{r} \sum_{j=1}^{r} \bar{f}_{ij} + \sum_{i=1}^{r} \sum_{j=1}^{r} \bar{e}_{ij} = 1, \quad (6)$$

$$0 \leq \bar{e}_{ij} \leq 1, \ 0 \leq \bar{f}_{ij} \leq 1, \ 0 \leq \bar{a}_i \leq 1, \quad (7)$$

$$\sum_{j=1}^{r} q_{ij} = 1, q_{ij} \geq 0. \quad (8)$$

The interpretation of (1)–(8) is intuitive. Objective (1) captures the tradeoff between revenue generation, and the cost of empty-car routing. Constraints (2)–(4) are flow-balance constraints. Constraint (5) states that for region i, either $\bar{a}_i = 1$ or $\bar{e}_{ii} = 0$, i.e. either availability is at 100% or the long-run fraction of empty cars at the station is zero.

The following are our main results. Theorems 2.1 establishes the connection between the fluid-based optimization problem and $(\tilde{E}^{(N)}, \tilde{F}^{(N)})$. Theorems 2.2 shows that asymptotically, the optimal static policy from the fluid-based optimization outperforms all state dependent policies.

THEOREM 2.1. *Let $q, \hat{e}, \hat{f}, \hat{a}$ be a feasible solution to the optimization problem in (1)–(8). Set $Q = q$. Assume $P_{ij} > 0$ for all $1 \leq i, j \leq r$ and $q_{ii} > 0$ for all $1 \leq i \leq r$. Then*

$$\tilde{F}^{(N)}(\infty) \Rightarrow \hat{f}, \quad (9)$$

$$\tilde{E}_{ij}^{(N)}(\infty) \Rightarrow \hat{e}_{ij}, \ 0 \leq i \neq j \leq 1, \quad (10)$$

$$\tilde{E}_{ii}^{(N)}(\infty) \Rightarrow 0, \ \text{for } i \text{ such that } \hat{a}_i < 1, \quad (11)$$

$$\sum_{i:\bar{a}_i=1} \tilde{E}_{ii}^{(N)}(\infty) \Rightarrow \sum_{i:\hat{a}_i=1} \hat{e}_{ii}, \quad (12)$$

and

$$\mathbb{P}(E_{ii}^{(N)}(\infty) > 0) \to \hat{a}_i, \ 0 \leq i \leq 1, \quad (13)$$

as $N \to \infty$.

THEOREM 2.2. *(a) Suppose $(\tilde{E}^{(N)}, \tilde{F}^{(N)})$ is irreducible under P and Q, where Q is a state-dependent empty-car routing policy. Let $(q^*, \bar{e}^*, \bar{f}^*, \bar{a}^*)$ be an optimal solution of the optimization problem in (1)–(8). Then*

$$\sum_{i=1}^{r} c_i \lambda_i A_i^{(N)} - \sum_{i=1}^{r} \sum_{j=1, j \neq i}^{r} \tilde{c}_{ij} \mathbb{E}\left[\tilde{E}_{ij}^{(N)}(\infty)\right]$$

$$\leq \sum_{i=1}^{r} c_i \lambda_i \bar{a}_i^* - \sum_{i=1}^{r} \sum_{j=1, j \neq i}^{r} \tilde{c}_{ij} \bar{e}_{ij}^*, N > 0.$$

(b) Let $(\tilde{E}^{(N)*}, \tilde{F}^{(N)*})$ denote the CTMC under the static routing policy q^*. If $P_{ij} > 0$ for all $1 \leq i, j \leq r$ and $q_{ii}^* > 0$ for all $1 \leq i \leq r$, then

$$\lim_{N \to \infty} \sum_{i=1}^{r} c_i \lambda_i A_i^{(N)*} - \sum_{i=1}^{r} \sum_{j=1, j \neq i}^{r} \tilde{c}_{ij} \mathbb{E}\left[\tilde{E}_{ij}^{(N)*}(\infty)\right]$$

$$= \sum_{i=1}^{r} c_i \lambda_i \bar{a}_i^* - \sum_{i=1}^{r} \sum_{j=1, j \neq i}^{r} \tilde{c}_{ij} \bar{e}_{ij}^*.$$

3 EVALUATION

In this section, we evaluate the convergence of the utility under the fluid-based policy to the fluid-based optimal solution, as N increases, on a nine-region network as shown in Figure 1, which was extracted from a data set released in the Di-Tech Challenge by the Didi Research Institute http://research.xiaojukeji.com/index_en.html. The nodes represent the regions, and the edge-weights are the estimated average travel times.

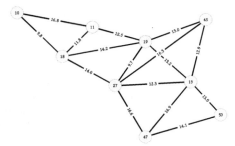

Figure 1: The nine-region network extracted from the DiDi dataset

We chose the utility function $U(\bar{a}) = \frac{\sum_{i=1}^{r} \lambda_i \bar{a}_i}{\sum_{i=1}^{r} \lambda_i}$, which is the probability that a passenger requesting a ride at *any* region is fulfilled. The utility function $U(\bar{a})$ can be retrieved by setting $c_i = \frac{1}{\sum_{i=1}^{r} \lambda_i}$ and $\tilde{c}_{ij} = 0$ in (1). Let Q^* be the optimal routing matrix from (2)–(8) with $U(\bar{a})$ and $a^* = U(\bar{a}^*)$ be the associated optimal system-wide availability. Let $a^{(N)} = U(A^{(N)})$ be the system-wide availability for the finite sized system with N cars under the optimal routing policy Q^*. Figure 2 shows that the convergence appears to be happening at a rate of $1/\sqrt{N}$.

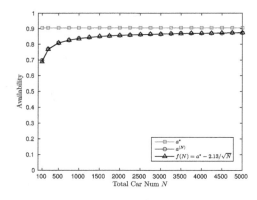

Figure 2: Convergence of the system-wide availability to its fluid-based optimal availability in the nine-region network.

REFERENCES

[1] F. Baskett, K. M. Chandy, R. R. Muntz, and F. G. Palacios. 1975. Open, closed and mixed networks of queues with different classes of customers. *Journal of the Association for Computing Machinery* 22 (1975), 248–260.

[2] A. Braverman, J. G. Dai, X. Liu, and L. Ying. 2016. Empty-car routing in ridesharing systems. *ArXiv e-prints* (Sept. 2016). arXiv:math.PR/1609.07219

Pseudo-Separation for Assessment of Structural Vulnerability of a Network

Alan Kuhnle
University of Florida
kuhnle@ufl.edu

Tianyi Pan
University of Florida
tianyi@cise.ufl.edu

Victoria G. Crawford
University of Florida
vcrawford01@ufl.edu

Md Abdul Alim
University of Florida
alim@cise.ufl.edu

My T. Thai
University of Florida
mythai@ufl.edu

ABSTRACT

Based upon the idea that network functionality is impaired if two nodes in a network are sufficiently separated in terms of a given metric, we introduce two combinatorial *pseudocut* problems generalizing the classical min-cut and multi-cut problems. We expect the pseudocut problems will find broad relevance to the study of network reliability. We comprehensively analyze the computational complexity of the pseudocut problems and provide three approximation algorithms for these problems.

Motivated by applications in communication networks with strict Quality-of-Service (QoS) requirements, we demonstrate the utility of the pseudocut problems by proposing a targeted vulnerability assessment for the structure of communication networks using QoS metrics; we perform experimental evaluations of our proposed approximation algorithms in this context.

KEYWORDS

Approximation algorithms; Network cutting problems

ACM Reference format:
Alan Kuhnle, Tianyi Pan, Victoria G. Crawford, Md Abdul Alim, and My T. Thai. 2017. Pseudo-Separation for Assessment of Structural Vulnerability of a Network. In *Proceedings of SIGMETRICS '17, Urbana-Champaign, IL, USA, June 5-9, 2017,* 2 pages.
https://doi.org/http://dx.doi.org/10.1145/3078505.3078538

1 INTRODUCTION

Many studies of network vulnerability, or the degree to which the functionality of a network may be disrupted by failures, have incorporated connectivity as a fundamental measure of network functionality [1, 2]. Whatever functionality a network may provide to a pair of nodes is usually absent if the pair is disconnected. In this work, we generalize the idea of network impairment resulting from disconnection of network elements to impairment upon sufficient separation in the network according to a given metric; that is, if $d(s, t) > T$ for two vertices s, t, distance metric d, and threshold T. As an example of the impairment of network functionality under

SIGMETRICS '17, June 5-9, 2017, Urbana-Champaign, IL, USA
© 2017 Copyright held by the owner/author(s).
ACM ISBN ACM ISBM 978-1-4503-5032-7/17/06.
https://doi.org/http://dx.doi.org/10.1145/3078505.3078538

sufficient separation, consider the Industrial Internet of Things (IIoT), which allows extensive monitoring and control of production facilities in real time [3]. However, the Quality-of-Service (QoS) requirements for control of production systems are very strict [4]. Thus, if two nodes in the IIoT network are sufficently separated in terms of the QoS metric, the network functionality is impaired.

Contributions: Based upon this idea of functionality impairment under sufficient separation, we introduce novel T-separation analogues to the the min-cut and multi-cut problem [5, 6], T-PCUT and T-MULTI-PCUT, respectively. These problems are formally defined in Section 2. In Section 3, we analyze the computational complexity of these two problems, and in Section 4, we present GEN, an $O(\log n)$-approximation algorithm, and FEN, a $(T + 1)$-approximation algorithm. In addition, we provide GEST, an efficient, randomized algorithm with probabilistic performance guarantee: with probability $1 - 1/n$, GEST returns a feasible solution with cost within ratio $O(\alpha\delta^T + \log k)$ of optimal, where k is the number of pairs to T-separate, δ is the maximum degree in the graph, and α is user-defined parameter in $(0, 1)$ which also impacts the running time of GEST. An experimental evaluation of these algorithms and a detailed discussion of related work is presented in the full version[1].

2 PROBLEM DEFINITIONS

In this section, we introduce the vertex versions of the pseudocut problems; the edge versions are presented in the full version. Let T be an arbitrary but fixed constant throughout this section. The problems will take as input a triple (G, c, d), where G is a directed graph $G = (V, E)$; $c : V \rightarrow \mathbf{R}^+$ is a cost function on vertices representing the difficulty of removing each node; and $d : E \rightarrow \mathbf{R}^+$ is a length function on edges. For example, $d(e)$ could be a QoS metric such as latency or packet loss on edge e. Although both c and d may be considered weight functions, we use *cost* for c and *length* for d to avoid confusion. The case when $c(v) = 1$ for all vertices is referred to as *uniform cost*, and the case when $d(e) = 1$ for all edges is referred to as *uniform length*. The distance $d(u, v)$ between two vertices is the length of the d-weighted, directed, and shortest path between u and v; the cost $c(W)$ of set W of a set of vertices is the sum of the costs of individual vertices in W.

PROBLEM 1 (MINIMUM T-PSEUDOCUT (T-PCUT)). *Given triple (G, c, d) and a pair (s, t) of vertices of G, determine a minimum cost set $W \subset V \backslash \{s, t\}$ of vertices such that $d(s, t) > T$ after the removal of W from G.*

---

[1]The full version of this paper is available at https://arxiv.org/abs/1704.04555

PROBLEM 2 (MINIMUM T-MULTI-PSEUDOCUT (T-MULTI-PCUT)). *Given triple (G, c, d), and a target set of pairs of vertices of G, $\mathcal{S} = \{(s_1, t_1), (s_2, t_2), \ldots, (s_k, t_k)\}$, determine a minimum cost set W of vertices such that $d(s_i, t_i) > T$ for all i after the removal of W from G.*

In the above two formulations, we emphasize that the threshold T is a fixed constant independent of the input. We will consider simple paths $p = p_0 p_1 \ldots p_l \in G$; that is, paths containing no cycles. Let $\mathcal{P}(s_i, t_i)$ denote the set of simple paths p between $(s_i, t_i) \in \mathcal{S}$ that satisfy the condition $d(p) \leq T$, and let $\mathcal{P} = \bigcup_{i=1}^{k} \mathcal{P}(s_i, t_i)$.

3 COMPUTATIONAL COMPLEXITY

In this section, we summarize our results from the full version on the computational complexity of the pseudocut problems. For uniform-length T-PCUT, we provide polynomial-time algoriths for specific special cases, although with arbitrary edge lengths the problem is shown to be NP-hard. For uniform length, cost T-MULTI-PCUT, an approximation-preserving from the vertex cover problem [7] exists.

PROPOSITION 3.1. *For $T \leq 3$, T-PCUT with uniform lengths and costs is solvable in polynomial time.*

PROPOSITION 3.2. *Let D be a constant, T-PCUT$(G, (s, t))$ be an instance of T-PCUT for some constant T with uniform lengths and uniform costs. If the maximum degree δ in G satisfies $\delta \leq D$, then the optimal solution W is computable in polynomial time.*

THEOREM 3.3. *Consider the decision version of 1-PCUT with uniform costs and arbitrary lengths; that is, given problem instance 1-PCUT$(G, (s, t))$ with uniform costs and arbitrary lengths, and given constant $D > 0$, determine if a solution $W \subset V$ exists with $|W| \leq D$. This problem is NP-complete.*

THEOREM 3.4. *Unless $P = NP$, there is no polynomial-time approximation to uniform length, cost T-MULTI-PCUT within a factor of 1.3606, for $T \geq 1$.*

4 APPROXIMATION ALGORITHMS

In this section, we present three approximation algorithms for arbitrary vertex cost T-MULTI-PCUT, when the length function on edges is bounded below: $d(e) > q_{min}$ for some constant $q_{min} > 0$. Let $T_0 = T/q_{min}$. Then, all paths in $\mathcal{P}$ can be enumerated in $O(n^{T_0})$. Furthermore, an optimal solution S of vertices must intersect every path in $\mathcal{P}$. Thus, T-MULTI-PCUT may be considered as a special case of the set covering problem [7], where the paths correspond to the elements to be covered and vertices correspond to sets. More details are presented in the full version.

Then, we have two approximation algorithms for set cover that apply: the greedy algorithm (GEN), choosing at each iteration the vertex covering the most paths in $\mathcal{P}$, and the frequency rounding algorithm (FEN) based upon the optimal solution to the linear program corresponding to the set cover instance [7]. The following theorems are proved in the full version.

THEOREM 4.1. *GEN achieves a performance guarantee of $O(\log n)$ with respect to the optimal solution with running time bounded by $O(kn^{T_0})$. Furthermore, for each n, there exists an instance of the single pair PCUT problem where GEN returns a solution of cost greater than a factor $\Omega(\log n)$ of the optimal.*

THEOREM 4.2. *FEN achieves a performance guarantee of $T_0 + 1$ with respect to the optimal solution.*

Although GEN, FEN both run in polynomial time, the enumeration of all paths at most length T may be very expensive. Therefore, we formulate a probabilistic approximation algorithm, GEST, which is similar to GEN except that GEST estimates which node intersects the most paths; to perform this estimation, GEST samples paths in the following way: for each pair $(s, t) \in \mathcal{S}$, a path beginning from s is sampled by randomly walking from s until the path exceeds the length T or until t is reached; if t is reached, the sampled path is *valid*. The number $\tau(S)$ of such paths a set S of vertices intersects is estimated using the probability of the path, which is computed iteratively: each step i in the random walk multiplies the probability of the path by $1/n_i$, where n_i is the number of available vertices at step i. If set S intersects a valid sampled path p, with $Pr(p) = \eta$, then the estimated number of paths between (s, t) that S intersects is increased by $1/\eta$. In the full version, we show that this estimator is unbiased and prove the following bound on the number of samples required to get a good estimate $\sigma(S)$.

LEMMA 4.3. *Let the number of paths sampled for each $(s, t) \in \mathcal{S}$ be at least $L = 3k^2 \log(2n^2)/2\alpha^2$, where $\alpha \in (0, 1)$. Then, given a set $S \subseteq V$ and δ as the maximum degree in G, the inequality $|\tau(S) - \sigma(S)| < \alpha \delta^{T_0}$ holds with probability at least $1 - 1/n^3$.*

Lemma 4.3 allows us to prove the following probabilistic performance guarantee for GEST. The proof is detailed in the full version.

THEOREM 4.4. *Given an instance $(G, c, d, \mathcal{S})$ of uniform vertex cost T-MULTI-PCUT whose length function d is bounded below, let δ be the maximum degree in G, and let $\alpha \in (0, 1)$. With probability at least $1 - 1/n$, GEST returns a feasible solution W with cost within ratio $O\left(\alpha \delta^{T_0} + \log |\mathcal{S}|\right)$ of optimal. The running time of GEST is $O(k^3 n \log(2n^2)/2\alpha^2)$.*

5 ACKNOWLEDGEMENTS

This work is supported in part by NSF grant CNS-1443905 and DTRA grant HDTRA1-14-1-0055.

REFERENCES

[1] Tony H Grubesic, Timothy C Matisziw, Alan T Murray, and Diane Snediker. Comparative Approaches for Assessing Network Vulnerability. *International Regional Science Review*, 31(1):88–112, 2008.

[2] Thang N. Dinh and My T. Thai. Network under joint node and link attacks: Vulnerability assessment methods and analysis. *IEEE/ACM Transactions on Networking*, 23(3):1001–1011, 2015.

[3] Ahmad-Reza Sadeghi, Christian Wachsmann, and Michael Waidner. Security and Privacy Challenges in Industrial Internet of Things. *Proceedings of the 52nd Annual Design Automation Conference on - DAC '15*, 17:1–6, 2015.

[4] Linus Thrybom and Gunnar Prytz. QoS in Switched Industrial Ethernet. *IEEE Conference on Emerging Technologies and Factory Automation*, 2009.

[5] Naveen Garg, Vijay V. Vazirani, and Mihalis Yannakakis. Multiway Cuts in Directed and Node Weighted Graphs. In *International Colloquium on Automata, Languages, and Programming.*, Berlin, 1994. Springer-Verlag.

[6] Tom Leighton and Satish Rao. Multicommodity max-flow min-cut theorems and their use in designing approximation algorithms. *Journal of the ACM*, 46(6):787–832, 1999.

[7] Vijay V Vazirani. *Approximation Algorithms*. Springer-Verlag Berlin Heidelberg, first edition, 2003.

On the Capacity Requirement for Arbitrary End-to-End Deadline and Reliability Guarantees in Multi-hop Networks

Han Deng
Texas A&M University
College Station, Texas 77840
hdeng@tamu.edu

I-Hong Hou
Texas A&M University
College Station, Texas 77840
ihou@tamu.edu

ABSTRACT

It has been shown that it is impossible to achieve both stringent end-to-end deadline and reliability guarantees in a large network without having complete information of all future packet arrivals. In order to maintain desirable performance in the presence of uncertainty of future packet arrivals, common practice is to add redundancy by increasing link capacities. This paper studies the amount of capacity needed to provide stringent performance guarantees and propose a low-complexity online algorithm. Without adding redundancy, we further propose a low-complexity order-optimal online policy for the network.

CCS CONCEPTS

• Networks → Packet scheduling;

KEYWORDS

Multi-hop Network; Online Scheduling; CompetitiveRatio; Capacity Performance Trade-off

ACM Reference format:
Han Deng and I-Hong Hou. 2017. On the Capacity Requirement for Arbitrary End-to-End Deadline and Reliability Guarantees in Multi-hop Networks. In *Proceedings of SIGMETRICS '17, June 5-9, 2017, Urbana-Champaign, IL, USA, , 2 pages.*
DOI: http://dx.doi.org/10.1145/3078505.3078540

1 INTRODUCTION

Many emerging safety-critical applications, such as Internet of Things (IoT) and Cyber-Physical Systems (CPS), require communication protocols that support strict end-to-end delay and reliability guarantees for all packets. In a typical scenario, when sensors detect unusual events that can cause system instability, they send out this information to actuators or control centers. This information needs to be delivered within a strict deadline for actuators or control centers to resolve the unusual events. The system can suffer from a critical fault when a small portion of packets fail to be delivered on time.

In the multi-hop network system, packet arrivals are time-varying and unpredictable. It is obvious that one cannot design the optimal network policies without obtaining complete knowledge of future packet arrivals and incurring high computation complexity. Therefore, practical solutions need to rely on online suboptimal policies. In order to maintain desirable performance using online suboptimal policies, current practice is to add redundancy into the system. During system deployment, the capacities of communication links are chosen to be larger than necessary. Such redundancy alleviates the negative impacts of suboptimal decisions by online policies. Using this approach, a critical question is to determine the amount of redundancy needed to provide the desirable performance guarantees. This paper aims to answer this question.

We formulate the problem as a linear programming problem and propose an online policy that achieves good performance in terms of competitive ratio using the primal-dual [1] method. We show that when there is no redundancy added to the system, the performance of our online policy is asymptotically better than that of the recent work by Mao et al. [2] when the size of the network increases. Next, we establish a theoretical lower bound of competitive ratio for all online policies. In addition, we propose an online policy that achieves order-optimal with fixed link capacity.

2 SYSTEM MODEL

We consider a network with multihop transmissions. The network is represented by a directed graph where each node represents a router and an edge from one node to another represents a link between the corresponding routers. Different links in the network may have different link capacities. Packets arrive at their respective source nodes following some unknown sequence. When a packet arrives at its source node, it specifies its destination and a deadline. At the beginning of each time slot, each node decides which packets to transmit over its links. The packet requests to be delivered to its destination before its specified deadline. Packets that are not delivered on time do not have any value, and can be dropped from the network. We aim to deliver as many packets on time as possible.

This material is based upon work supported in part by the U. S. Army Research Laboratory and the U. S. Army Research Office under contract/grant number W911NF-15-1-0279 and NPRP Grant 8-1531-2-651 of Qatar National Research Fund (a member of Qatar Foundation).
Full paper can be found: https://arxiv.org/pdf/1704.04857.pdf.

It is obvious that designing the optimal routing and scheduling policy requires complete knowledge of all packet arrivals in advance. In fact, a recent work has shown that, when the longest path between a source node and a destination node is L, no online policy can guarantee to deliver more than $\frac{1}{log_2 L}$ as many packets as the optimal solution. Such performance guarantee is usually unacceptable for practical applications, especially when the size of the network is large.

In order to achieve good performance for online policies in the presence of unknown future arrivals, we consider the scenario where service providers can increase link capacities by, for example, upgrading network infrastructures. We assume the link capacities are all increased by R times.

To evaluate the performance of online policies, we define a competitive ratio that incorporates the increase in capacities:

Definition 2.1. Given a sequence of packet arrivals, let Γ_{opt} be the optimal number of delivered packets with original link capacity, and $\Gamma_\eta(R)$ be the number of packets that are delivered under an online policy η when the link capacities are increased by R times. The online policy η is said to be (R, ρ)-*competitive* if $\Gamma_{opt}/\Gamma_\eta(R) \leq \rho$, for any sequence of packet arrivals.

3 RESULT

We have three main results in the paper.

3.1 An Online Algorithm and Its Competitive Ratio

We propose an low-complexity online algorihtm based on primal-dual method. It suggests a route for an arriving packet by considering all link usage on any possible route. When a route is chosen for the packet, all links along the path will update the link usages according to the method we propose in the algorithm. We have the following theorem for its competitive ratio.

THEOREM 3.1. *Let C_{min} be the minimum link capacity, $d_{min} := (1 + 1/C_{min})^{RC_{min}}$, and L be the longest path between a source node and a destination node. Our algorithm is $(R, 1 + \frac{L}{d_{min}-1})$-competitive, which converges to $(R, 1 + \frac{L}{e^R - 1})$-competitive, as $C_{min} \to \infty$.*

3.2 A Theoretical Lower Bound for Competitive Ratio

We derive a lower bound on the performance of all online algorithms.

THEOREM 3.2. *Any online algorithm cannot be better than $(R, 1 + \frac{L - 2e^R}{(L+1)e^R - L})$-competitive.*

Therefore, to guarantee to deliver at least $1 - \frac{1}{\theta}$ as many packets as the optimal solution, the capacity requirement of our policy is at most $\ln(L + 2\theta - 1)$ away from the lower bound. Suppose we fix the ratio between L and θ, and let them both go to infinity, then we have $(\ln L + \ln \theta)/(\ln L + \ln \theta - \ln(L + 2\theta - 1)) \to 2$. Therefore, when both L and θ are

large, our policy at most requires twice as much capacity as the theoretical lower bound.

3.3 An Order-Optimal Online Policy with Original Capacity

We propose an optimal online algorithm which is $(1, O(\log L))$-competitive when the link capacity cannot be increased. The online algorithm uses a similar process to choose routes but it updates link usages with a different method. Comparing the updating process with the previous online algorithm, we find it to increase much slower when the link is lightly loaded and increase much faster when the link is heavy loaded. Such mechanism ensures that more packets with long routes can be accepted, especially when the network is lightly loaded.

4 A HEURISTIC FOR DISTRIBUTED IMPLEMENTATION

The two algorithms that we have proposed so far are both centralized algorithms. Specifically, when a packet arrives at a node, the node needs to have complete knowledge of all link usages at different time to find a route. Such information is usually infeasible to obtain. Thus we propose a distributed heuristics based on the design of our centralized algorithm.

Our distributed heuristic is composed of two parts: First, when a packet arrives at a node, the node determines a suggested schedule based on statistics of past system history. This suggested schedule consists of the route for forwarding the packet, as well as a local deadline for each link. After determining the suggested schedule, the node simply forwards it to the first link of the route. On the other hand, when a link receives a packet along with a suggested schedule, the link tries to forward the packet to the next link in the suggested schedule before its local deadline. The link drops the packet when it cannot forward the packet on time.

5 CONCLUSIONS

In this paper, we study the multi-hop network scheduling problem with end-to-end deadline and hard transmission rate requirement. Given the capacity of each link in the network, we aim to find out how much capacity we need to increase to guarantee the required ratio of packets can be successfully transmitted to its destination before its deadline without knowing the packet arrival sequences in advance. We propose two centralized online algorithms which both have better performance than that presented in [2]. We also propose a heuristic for distributed implementation based on the first online algorithm.

REFERENCES

[1] Niv Buchbinder and Joseph (Seffi) Naor. 2009. The Design of Competitive Online Algorithms via a Primal: Dual Approach. *Found. Trends Theor. Comput. Sci.* 3, 2–3 (Feb. 2009), 93–263. DOI:https://doi.org/10.1561/0400000024
[2] Z. Mao, C. E. Koksal, and N. B. Shroff. 2016. Optimal Online Scheduling With Arbitrary Hard Deadlines in Multihop Communication Networks. *IEEE/ACM Transactions on Networking* 24, 1 (Feb 2016), 177–189. DOI: https://doi.org/10.1109/TNET.2014.2363136

Optimizing Speculative Execution of Deadline-Sensitive Jobs in Cloud

Maotong Xu, Sultan Alamro, Tian Lan, and Suresh Subramaniam
Department of Electrical and Computer Engineering
The George Washington University
{htfy8927, alamro, tlan, suresh}@gwu.edu

ABSTRACT

In this paper, we bring various speculative scheduling strategies together under a unifying optimization framework, which defines a new metric, Probability of Completion before Deadlines (PoCD), to measure the probability that MapReduce jobs meet their desired deadlines. We propose an optimization problem to jointly optimize PoCD and execution cost in different strategies. Three strategies are prototyped on Hadoop MapReduce and evaluated against two baseline strategies using experiments. A 78% net utility increase with up to 94% PoCD and 12% cost improvement is achieved.

KEYWORDS

MapReduce; Straggler; Speculative Strategy; PoCD

1 INTRODUCTION

Hadoop, built on the MapReduce programming model, has been widely employed by giant companies such as Facebook, Google, and Yahoo! for processing big data. It splits large amount of data into blocks and distributes them across machines to process the data in parallel. However, such parallel data processing framework is susceptible to heavy tails in response time, and job execution times could be adversely impacted by a few slow tasks, called stragglers. These stragglers are inevitable in the cloud environment due to resource contentions and hardware/software errors, and they could result in high latency and impact the overall performance of deadline-sensitive cloud applications.

Both proactive and reactive techniques are proposed to mitigate stragglers. Dolly [1] is a proactive cloning approach. It launches multiple attempts for each task, and the task completes when the earliest attempt finishes. LATE [2] presents a scheduling algorithm to check if the task is a straggler, and launch speculative attempts for each straggler. However, no existing work provides any guarantee to meet application deadlines.

Meeting desired deadlines is crucial since cloud applications are becoming increasingly deadline-sensitive. In this paper, we present an optimization framework for three straggler mitigation strategies– Clone, Speculative-Restart, and Speculative-Resume. For each MapReduce job, the optimization finds the optimal number r of speculative/clone attempts for each strategy to exploit the PoCD and cost tradeoff. The optimization framework unifies all three

SIGMETRICS '17, June 05-09, 2017, Urbana- Champaign, IL, USA
© 2017 Copyright held by the owner/author(s). ACM ISBN 978-1-4503-5032-7/17/06.
DOI: http://dx.doi.org/10.1145/3078505.3078541

strategies and maximizes a *net utility* that is defined as a utility function of r. The utility function ($U(r)$) consists of PoCD ($R(r)$), i.e., the probability of meeting job deadlines, and total execution cost, which is measured by the total expected (virtual) machine time ($E(T)$). More specifically,

$$U(r) = \log(R(r) - R_{\min}) - \theta \cdot C \cdot E(T), \qquad (1)$$

where $R_{\min}$ is a minimum required PoCD, and T is the execution time of a job. θ is the tradeoff between the PoCD and cost, and C is the usage-based VM price per unit time. To the best of our knowledge, this is the first work to provide a systematic study of various scheduling strategies and to offer an analytical framework for joint optimization of the probability of meeting deadlines and the associated execution cost.

We evaluate Clone, Speculative-Restart, and Speculative-Resume strategies and compare them against two baseline strategies including default Hadoop without speculation (Hadoop-NS), and default Hadoop with speculation (Hadoop-S), in our cloud testbed consisting of 80 nodes. Using two classic benchmarks, WordCount and Sort, we show that Speculative-Resume outperforms the baseline algorithms by an average of 78% in net utility improvement, which results from a significant PoCD increase (up to 94%) and/or cost reduction (up to 12%), while the improvement is even higher for more stringent application deadlines.

2 BACKGROUND AND SYSTEM MODEL

Suppose M jobs are submitted to a datacenter, where job i is associated with a deadline D_i and consists of N_i tasks for $i = 1, 2, \ldots, M$. Job i meets the deadline if all N_i tasks are processed before D_i. A task whose execution time exceeds D_i is considered as a straggler. To mitigate stragglers, we launch r_i extra attempts of each task along with an original attempt, and a task is completed as long as one of the attempts is successfully executed. We denote the (random) execution time of attempt k of job i's task j as $T_{i,j,k}$. Thus, we define job i's completion time T_i and task completion time $T_{i,j}$ by:

$$T_i = \max_{j=1, \ldots, N_i} T_{i,j}, \text{ where } T_{i,j} = \min_{k=1, \ldots, r_i+1} T_{i,j,k}, \ \forall j. \qquad (2)$$

[3–5] model the execution times of tasks by using the Pareto distribution. Following these papers, we assume the execution time $T_{i,j,k}$ of each attempt follows a Pareto distribution with parameters $t_{\min}$, and β, where $t_{\min}$ is the minimum execution time and β is the exponent, and the execution times of different attempts are independent. We use progress score, i.e., the percentage of workload processed at a given time t, to determine if extra attempts are needed. More specifically, the estimated execution time equals the sum of the amount of time to launch the task and the amount of

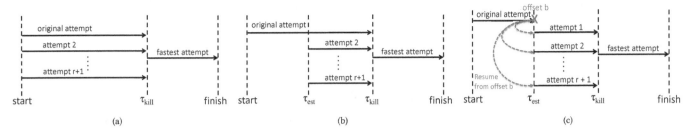

Figure 1: (a) Clone Strategy, (b) Speculative-Restart Strategy, (c) Speculative-Resume Strategy.

time used for processing data divided by the progress score. In the following, we describe the details of the three strategies.

Clone Strategy. Under this strategy, $r + 1$ attempts of each task are launched at the beginning, including one original attempt and r extra attempts. At time τ_{kill}, the progress scores of all attempts are checked, and the attempt with the best progress score is left running, while the other r attempts are killed to save machine running time. Figure 1(a) illustrates the Clone strategy for a task.

Speculative-Restart (S-Restart) Strategy. Under this strategy, one attempt (original) of each task is launched at the beginning. The attempt completion time is estimated at time τ_{est}. If the estimated attempt completion time exceeds D, r extra attempts are launched to process data from the beginning. The progress scores of all attempts are checked at time τ_{kill}, and the attempt with the smallest estimated completion time is left running, while the other r attempts are killed. Figure 1(b) illustrates the Speculative-Restart strategy for a task whose estimated execution time exceeds D.

Speculative-Resume (S-Resume) Strategy. This strategy is similar to the Speculative-Restart strategy in its straggler detection. The difference is that at time τ_{est}, the straggler is killed and $r + 1$ attempts are launched for the straggling task. These attempts, however, do not reprocess the data that has already been processed by the original attempt; they process the data starting from the byte after the last byte processed by the original straggler task. The progress scores of all attempts are checked at time τ_{kill}, and the attempt with the smallest estimated completion time is left running while the other r attempts are killed. Figure 1(c) illustrates the Speculative-Resume strategy for a task whose estimated execution time exceeds D. The b denotes the byte offset from which extra attempts start processing.

3 EVALUATION

We compare Hadoop-NS, Hadoop-S, Clone, S-Restart, and S-Resume with respect to PoCD, cost, and net utility. In each of the three strategies, the optimal number, r_{opt}, of clone/speculative attempts is found by solving our proposed net utility optimization. We execute 100 MapReduce jobs, where each job consists of 10 tasks, on our testbed consisting of 80 nodes, where each node has 8 vCPUs and 2GB memory. The physical servers are connected to a GigE switch and the link bandwidth is 1Gbps. We evaluate the strategies by using the Map phases of two classic benchmarks, WordCount and Sort. WordCount is a CPU-bound application and Sort is an I/O-bound application. We download 1.2GB workload for WordCount from Wikipedia, and generate 1.2GB workload for Sort by using the RandomWriter application. We measure the PoCD by

Table 1: Comparison of different strategies.

	Metrics	H-NS	H-S	Clone	S-Restart	S-Resume
	PoCD	0.50	0.78	0.97	0.96	0.94
Sort	Cost(e-3, $)	2.15	2.39	3.63	3.15	2.75
	Utility	$-\infty$	-0.65	-0.47	-0.46	-0.45
	PoCD	0.46	0.64	0.81	0.79	0.85
WC	Cost(e-3, $)	3.56	4.10	5.67	4.64	3.60
	Utility	$-\infty$	-0.90	-0.32	-0.29	-0.20

calculating the percentage of jobs that completed before their deadlines and the cost by the average job running time (i.e., VM time required), assuming a fixed price per unit VM time that is obtained from Amazon EC2 average spot price ($C = 0.009\$/hr$). In all experiments, we set $\theta \cdot C = 0.0001$ and solve the corresponding net utility optimization. The deadlines are set to 200 sec and 270 sec for Sort and WordCount, respectively. For our three strategies, τ_{est} and τ_{kill} equal 60 sec and 120 sec, respectively. For net utility, since we use the PoCD of Hadoop-NS as R_{min}, its utility is negative infinity.

Table 1 summarizes the corresponding PoCD and cost in the optimal solutions, and compares the performance of the five strategies in terms of the overall net utility. Results show that our three strategies outperform Hadoop-NS and Hadoop-S by up to 78% on net utility value. In particular, the three strategies can improve PoCD by up to 94% and 33% over Hadoop-NS and Hadoop-S, respectively, while S-Resume introduces little additional cost compared with Hadoop-NS and Hadoop-S. This significant improvement comes from not only launching multiple attempts for stragglers, but also maintaining only the fastest attempt at τ_{kill}, thereby introducing limited execution time overhead.

4 ACKNOWLEDGEMENT

This work was supported in part by NSF grant 1320226.

REFERENCES

[1] G. Ananthanarayanan, A. Ghodsi, S. Shenker, and I. Stoica, "Effective straggler mitigation: Attack of the clones," in *Presented as part of the 10th USENIX Symposium on Networked Systems Design and Implementation (NSDI 13)*, 2013, pp. 185–198.

[2] M. Zaharia, A. Konwinski, A. D. Joseph, R. H. Katz, and I. Stoica, "Improving mapreduce performance in heterogeneous environments." in *OSDI*, vol. 8, no. 4, 2008, p. 7.

[3] G. Ananthanarayanan, M. C.-C. Hung, X. Ren, I. Stoica, A. Wierman, and M. Yu, "Grass: trimming stragglers in approximation analytics," in *11th USENIX Symposium on Networked Systems Design and Implementation (NSDI 14)*, 2014, pp. 289–302.

[4] D. Wang, G. Joshi, and G. Wornell, "Using straggler replication to reduce latency in large-scale parallel computing," *ACM SIGMETRICS Performance Evaluation Review*, vol. 43, no. 3, pp. 7–11, 2015.

[5] X. Ren, G. Ananthanarayanan, A. Wierman, and M. Yu, "Hopper: Decentralized speculation-aware cluster scheduling at scale," *ACM SIGCOMM Computer Communication Review*, vol. 45, no. 4, pp. 379–392, 2015.

A Spot Capacity Market to Increase Power Infrastructure Utilization in Multi-Tenant Data Centers

Mohammad A. Islam
University of California, Riverside

Xiaoqi Ren
California Institute of Technology

Shaolei Ren
University of California, Riverside

Adam Wierman
California Institute of Technology

1 INTRODUCTION

Scaling up power infrastructures to accommodate growing data center demand is one of the biggest challenges faced by data center operators today. It incurs a huge capital expense of US$10-25 to build each watt of IT critical power capacity. Additional constraints, such as local grid capacity and long time-to-market cycle, are also limiting the data center capacity expansion, as attested to by the recent data center supply shortfall in Silicon Valley.

Traditionally, data center power infrastructure is sized to support the servers' maximum aggregate power demand. Nonetheless, the power demands of servers rarely peak simultaneously, thus resulting in a low average utilization of the scarce power capacity.

More recently, data center operators have sought to overcome this inefficiency by aggressively using capacity oversubscription, i.e., by deploying more servers than what the power and/or cooling capacity allows and applying peak shaving techniques to handle the resulting emergencies [1]. However, data center power infrastructure is still largely under-utilized today, wasting more than 15% of the capacity on average. This is not due to the lack of data center capacity demand, but due to the fluctuation of the aggregate server power demand that does not always stay at high levels, whereas the infrastructure is provisioned to sustain a high demand. Consequently, there exists a varying amount of unused power capacity over time, which we refer to as *spot (power) capacity*. Fig. 1 illustrates the fluctuating power usage and resulting spot capacity in a large server cluster.

Spot capacity is common in data centers and, if properly utilized, can improve application performances at runtime. For example, recent studies have proposed to dynamically allocate spot capacity to servers/racks for performance boosting via power routing [2] and "soft fuse" [3].

Importantly, all the prior research on exploiting spot capacity for improving performance has focused on an owner-operated data center, where the operator fully controls the servers. In contrast, *our goal is to develop an approach for exploiting spot capacity in multi-tenant data centers*. Multi-tenant data centers (also commonly called colocation data centers) host multiple tenants in a shared facility, each managing their *own* physical servers while the operator is only responsible for non-IT infrastructure support (like power and

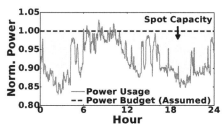

Figure 1: Power trace of a production server cluster in a top-brand IT company.

cooling). There are nearly 2,000 multi-tenant data centers in the U.S., serving almost all industry sectors.

The potential value of spot capacity in multi-tenant data centers parallels that in owner-operated data centers. Concretely, in practice, more than 50% of the servers in data centers run delay-tolerant workloads (like batch data processing) [1] and hence are well poised to opportunistically utilize spot capacity for performance improvement. Additionally, the operator can make extra profit by offering spot capacity to tenants on demand. Despite these benefits, exploiting spot capacity is more challenging and requires a significantly different approach in multi-tenant data centers than in owner-operated data centers, because the operator has no control over tenants' servers, let alone the knowledge of which tenants need spot capacity and by how much.

In this abstract, we present a novel market approach, called Spot Data Center capacity management (SpotDC), which leverages demand function bidding and dynamically allocates spot capacity to tenants' racks to improve performance. Our work is motivated by other spot markets (e.g., cognitive radio and Amazon EC2). However, market design for spot power in multi-tenant data centers has a variety of multifaceted challenges. First, spot capacity is allocated to tenants on a rack level, but the operator does not know when/which racks need spot capacity and by how much. Second, tenants' rack-level power usage can vary flexibly to achieve different performances, but extracting the *elastic* spot capacity demand at scale at runtime can be very challenging, especially in a large data center with thousands of racks. Finally, practical constraints (e.g., multi-level power capacity and heat density) require the operator to set market prices in a new way.

Our design of SpotDC addresses each of these challenges. First, it has a low overhead: only soliciting four bidding parameters for each rack that needs spot capacity. Second, it quickly computes spot capacity allocation under practical constraints, without compromising reliability. Finally, as demonstrated in realistic settings, SpotDC benefits both the tenants and the operator: tenants improve

SIGMETRICS '17, June 5-9, 2017, Urbana-Champaign, IL, USA
© 2017 Copyright held by the owner/author(s).
ACM ISBN ACM ISBN 978-1-4503-5032-7/17/06.
https://doi.org/http://dx.doi.org/10.1145/3078505.3078542

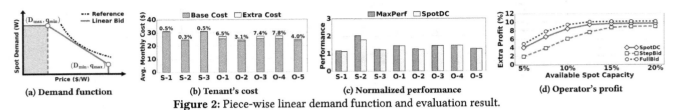

Figure 2: Piece-wise linear demand function and evaluation result.

performance by 1.2–1.8x (on average) at a marginal cost increase, while the operator can increase its profit by 9.7%.

2   DESIGN OF SPOTDC

The core of SpotDC is to leverage a new demand function bidding approach to extract tenants' rack-level spot capacity demand elasticity at runtime.

Demand function captures how the demand varies as a function of the price. To allocate spot capacity, the operator needs to know tenants' rack-wise demand functions for spot capacity at runtime. One might think that the operator can predict tenants' rack-level spot capacity demand functions, but this is very difficult because the demand can be highly dynamic and there can be hundreds or even thousands of racks. Another straightforward approach is to solicit tenant's complete rack-level demand curve under all possible prices (labeled as "Reference" in Fig. 2a), but this has a high communication overhead and is rarely used in real markets.

Demand function bidding. In practice, *parameterized* demand function bidding is commonly applied in different markets, such as Amazon EC2. Here, we propose a new parameterized demand function which, as illustrated by "Linear Bid" in Fig. 2a, *approximates* the actual demand curve using three line segments: first, a horizontal segment: tenant specifies its maximum spot capacity demand for a rack as well as the market price it is willing to pay; second, a linearly decreasing segment: the demand decreases linearly as the market price increases; and third, a vertical segment: the last segment indicates tenant's maximum acceptable price and the corresponding minimum demand. As shown in Fig. 2a, our piece-wise linear demand function for rack r is uniquely determined by four parameters: $\mathbf{b}_r = \{(D_{\max,r}, q_{\min,r}), (D_{\min,r}, q_{\max,r})\}$, where $D_{\max,r}$ and $D_{\min,r}$ are the maximum and minimum spot capacity demand, and $q_{\min,r}$ and $q_{\max,r}$ are the corresponding prices, respectively.

Our proposed demand function is simple yet can reasonably extract tenants' demand elasticity. In fact, it is a demand function widely studied for theoretical analysis. It also represents a *midpoint* between soliciting the complete demand curve and StepBid used by Amazon, which is simpler but cannot extract spot capacity demand elasticity (i.e., a tenant's spot capacity demand can only be either 100% or 0% satisfied). Our experiment results show that, using our demand function, the operator's profit is much higher than that using StepBid and also fairly close to the optimal profit when the complete demand curve is solicited.

Spot capacity allocation. The following three steps describe the spot capacity allocation process.

Step 1: *Demand function bidding.* Participating tenants decide, at their own discretion, bidding parameters for each rack that needs spot capacity and submit the bids to the operator.

Step 2: *Market clearing.* Upon collecting the bids, the operator sets the market price $q(t)$ to maximize profit subject to multi-level power and heat density constraints. This can be done very quickly through a simple search over the feasible price range.

Step 3: *Actual spot capacity allocation.* Given the market price $q(t)$ plugged into the demand function, each tenant knows its per-rack spot capacity and can use additional power up to the allocated spot capacity.

3   EVALUATION

We build a scaled-down testbed with 10 tenants grouped into two clusters. We consider delay-sensitive web search and web service workloads, as well as delay-tolerant Hadoop and graph analysis workloads. We model each tenant's power and performance to devise their demand bidding strategies for different workloads in order to improve performances at a low cost. We use real-world traces and conduct a one-month long simulation to evaluate SpotDC.

Figs. 2b and 2c show the additional cost incurred by each tenant participating in SpotDC and the corresponding performance improvement, respectively. Here, the base cost is tenant's power-related cost without SpotDC. The performance is normalized to that without SpotDC, while MaxPerf assumes a complete control of tenants' servers to allocate spot capacity for total performance maximization as if in an owner-operated data center. We see that for a marginal cost increase, the participating tenants are able to significantly improve their performance. Fig. 2d shows that the operator can make extra profit by exploiting spot capacity using SpotDC. We also see that SpotDC outperforms StepBid in terms of the operator's profit and is very close to FullBid that solicits a complete demand curve from each tenant.

To conclude, SpotDC is a novel market approach for exploiting spot capacity to increase power infrastructure utilization in multi-tenant data centers and turn spot capacity into a "win-win" resource: the operator makes additional profit, while the tenants improve performance at a low cost.

ACKNOWLEDGMENTS

This work was supported in part by the U.S. NSF under grants CNS-1551661, CNS-1565474, ECCS-1610471, AitF-1637598 and CNS-1518941, and the Resnick Sustainability Institute at Caltech.

REFERENCES

[1] M. A. Islam, X. Ren, S. Ren, A. Wierman, and X. Wang, "A market approach for handling power emergencies in multi-tenant data center," in *HPCA*, 2016.
[2] S. Pelley, D. Meisner, P. Zandevakili, T. F. Wenisch, and J. Underwood, "Power routing: Dynamic power provisioning in the data center," in *ASPLOS*, 2010.
[3] S. Govindan, J. Choi, B. Urgaonkar, and A. Sivasubramaniam, "Statistical profiling-based techniques for effective power provisioning in data centers," in *EuroSys*, 2009.

Hour-Ahead Offering Strategies in Electricity Market for Power Producers with Storage and Intermittent Supply

Lin Yang[*]
The Chinese University of Hong Kong
yl015@ie.cuhk.edu.hk

Mohammad H. Hajiesmaili
Johns Hopkins University
The Chinese University of Hong Kong
hajiesmaili@jhu.edu

Hanling Yi
The Chinese University of Hong Kong
yh014@ie.cuhk.edu.hk

Minghua Chen
The Chinese University of Hong Kong
minghua@ie.cuhk.edu.hk

ABSTRACT

This paper proposes online offering strategies for a storage-assisted renewable power producer that participates in hour-ahead electricity market. The online strategy determines the offering price and volume, while no exact or stochastic future information is available in a time-coupled setting in the presence of the storage. The proposed online strategy achieves the best possible competitive ratio of $O(\log \theta)$, where θ is the ratio between the maximum and minimum clearing prices. Trace-driven experiments demonstrate that the proposed strategy achieves close-to-optimal performance.

CCS CONCEPTS

•**Hardware → Smart grid;** •**Theory of computation →** *Online algorithms;* Scheduling algorithms;

KEYWORDS

Storage-assisted renewable power producer; hour-ahead electricity market; offering strategy; competitive online algorithm design

ACM Reference format:
Lin Yang, Mohammad H. Hajiesmaili, Hanling Yi, and Minghua Chen. 2017. Hour-Ahead Offering Strategies in Electricity Market for Power Producers with Storage and Intermittent Supply. In *Proceedings of SIGMETRICS '17, June 5–9, 2017, Urbana-Champaign, IL, USA, , 2 pages.*
DOI: http://dx.doi.org/10.1145/3078505.3078543

1 INTRODUCTION

In this paper, we consider a scenario in which a Storage-assisted Renewable GENeration COmpany (srGENCO), like other traditional generation companies, participates in hour-ahead electricity market by submitting its offer. After receiving the offers, the market operator matches the offers with the bids from the demand-side and determines a clearing price. If the offering price of srGENCO is less than the clearing price, its offering volume is considered as the *commitment* to the market for the next hour. Fig. 1 demonstrates

---

[*]The first two authors contributed equally to this work.

the scenario in this paper. This work focuses on designing profit maximizing offering strategies, i.e., the strategies that, with the goal of maximizing the profit, determine the offering price and volume, for srGENCO that participates in hour-ahead market.

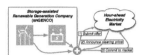

Figure 1: The scenario

Finding profit maximization offering strategy for a renewable producer without storage is nontrivial due to the inherent uncertainty of the renewables and dynamics in the market clearing price. In the presence of storage, the offering strategy is even more challenging because of the additional design space enabled by the storage. More specifically, srGENCO can use the storage absorb the uncertainty of renewables and to compensate for the slots that the renewable output cannot fulfill the commitment. However, the storage provides another economic advantage. That is, it can shift the energy through absorbing the renewable output during low price periods, and then discharging during high price periods. In this way, designing profit maximization offering strategy in the presence of storage comes with wider design space than those without the storage and potentially can bring more profit for srGENCO.

We formulate an optimization problem with the objective of maximizing the long-term profit of srGENCO. The future inputs to the problem, i.e., the renewable output and the clearing price, however, are unknown for srGENCO when submitting offer. This emphasizes the need for online solution design which is challenging, since the problem is coupled across time due to the evolution of the storage. We note that some similar problems have been studied in literature using stochastic optimization approaches [1], however, the solution approach in this paper is different since it has no assumption on the stochastic modeling of the future input. Our work could be considered as an extension of conversion problems [3].

Contribution. We propose sOffer, a simple online offering strategy, in which the offering strategy is designed using a piecewise exponential/constant function of the renewable output and the current storage level. The sOffer achieves the best possible competitive ratio of $O(\log \theta)$, where θ is the ratio between the maximum and minimum clearing prices. We refer to the full version of this paper [4] for detailed explanation.

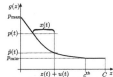

Figure 2: Calculating $x(t)$ when $p(t) > \hat{p}(t)$.

2 MODEL AND PROBLEM FORMULATION

We consider a time-slotted model, such that the time horizon T is chopped into multiple slots with equal length, e.g., 1 hour. Shortly before slot t, SRGENCO along with other participants submits its offer, for the next slot. We assume that SRGENCO knows the values of market clearing price $p_{\min} \le p(t) \le p_{\max}$ and renewable output $u(t) \ge 0$ for the coming slot. Extensions to the case in which neither clearing price nor renewable output is not known is given in [4]. Different from [1], we do not have any assumptions on the stochastic modeling of clearing price and renewable output beyond the coming slot. Since it is assumed that the clearing price is known, by offering strategy we mean the way that SRGENCO determines its offering (commitment) volume, denoted as $x(t) \ge 0$.

Storage Model: We denote the maximum capacity of storage system of SRGENCO by C and let ρ_c and ρ_d be its maximum charging and discharge rates, respectively. In addition, let $z(t) \in [0, C]$ be the storage level at the *beginning* of slot t. Given the renewable output $u(t)$ and the commitment volume $x(t)$, the evolution of the storage level of SRGENCO is given by

$$z(t+1) = \Big[z(t) + x_c(t) - x_d(t) \Big]_C,$$

where $x_c(t) = \min\big\{\rho_c, [u(t)-x(t)]^+\big\}$ and $x_d(t) = \min\big\{\rho_d, [x(t)-u(t)]^+\big\}$ are the charging and discharging amounts of the storage at slot t. Moreover, $[.]^+$ and $[.]_C$ define the projections onto the positive orthant and set $C = [0, C]$, respectively.

Now, we cast the simplified offering strategy problem sOSP as

$$\text{sOSP} \quad \max \quad \sum_{t \in \mathcal{T}} p(t)x(t)$$
$$\text{s.t.} \quad x(t) \le \min\{z(t), \rho_d\} + u(t),$$
$$z(t+1) = \Big[z(t) + x_c(t) - x_d(t) \Big]_C,$$
$$\text{var}: \quad x(t) \ge 0, t \in \mathcal{T},$$

where the first constraint ensures that the feasibility of offering amount. The second constraint involves the evolution of the storage.

3 ALGORITHM DESIGN

We design our algorithm following an *adaptive threshold-based* strategy, where the algorithm adaptively changes the offering volume based on the current storage level and the clearing price. The main idea is to construct a function $g(z) : [0, C] \to [p_{\min}, p_{\max}]$. The input to function $g(\cdot)$ is the aggregation of the incoming renewable supply $u(t)$ and the current storage level $z(t)$, projected into the capacity of the storage. Given function $g(z)$ the strategy works as follows. It first calculates $\hat{p}(t) = g(z^+(t))$ as the candidate offering price for $z^+(t) = \min\big[z(t) + \min\{u(t), \rho_c\}\big]_C$ as the storage level after absorbing renewable output. Since SRGENCO knows the cleating price $p(t)$ it can finds the offering volume $x(t)$ as follows:

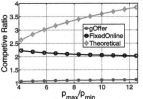

Figure 3: Competitive ratio as a function of price volatility

$$x(t) = \begin{cases} [u(t) - \rho_c]^+, & \text{if } \hat{p}(t) > p(t), \\ z(t) + u(t) - \min\{c^{\text{th}}, z(t) + \rho_c\}, & \text{if } \hat{p}(t) = p(t) = p_{\min}, \\ z(t) + u(t) - \min\{\hat{g}^{-1}(p(t)), z(t) + \rho_c\}, & \text{if } \hat{p}(t) < p(t), \end{cases}$$

An illustration of how offering volume is calculated is shown in Fig. 2. The following theorem characterizes the optimal function $g(\cdot)$ that leads to the best possible competitive ratio, for sOffer as the strategy that determines the offering volume as above.

THEOREM 3.1. *By setting $g(z)$ as*

$$g(z) = \begin{cases} p_{\min} e^{\frac{(c^{\text{th}}-z)c^{\text{th}}}{C(C-c^{\text{th}})}} & \text{if } z \le c^{\text{th}}, \\ p_{\min} & z \ge c^{\text{th}}. \end{cases} \tag{1}$$

where c^{th} is

$$c^{\text{th}} = C - \frac{(2 + \log\theta)C - \sqrt{\log^2\theta + 4\log\theta C}}{2} > 0, \tag{2}$$

and $\theta = p_{\max}/p_{\min}$. In addition,

$$CR(\text{sOffer}) = \frac{(2 + \log\theta) + \sqrt{\log^2\theta + 4\log\theta}}{2}. \tag{3}$$

4 SIMULATIONS

Using data from PJM energy market, we evaluate the performance of our algorithm in Fig. 3. We measure the empirical competitive ratio of FixedOnline [2], that determines the offering volume based on a fixed threshold, and gOffer (the general version of sOffer where neither clearing price nor renewable output are known [4]), and show the theoretical competitive ratio. The result depicts that (i) gOffer is robust to price fluctuation; (ii) gOffer is superior to FixedOnline; (iii) it works much better than theoretical bound.

ACKNOWLEDGMENT

Mohammad Hajiesmaili would like to thank Enrique Mallada for his helpful comments and financial support. The work presented in this paper was supported by the University Grants Committee of the Hong Kong Special Administrative Region, China (Theme-based Research Scheme Project No. T23-407/13-N).

REFERENCES

[1] D. R. Jiang and W. B. Powell. Optimal hour-ahead bidding in the real-time electricity market with battery storage using approximate dynamic programming. *INFORMS Journal on Computing*, 27(3):525–543, 2015.
[2] J. Lorenz, K. Panagiotou, and A. Steger. Optimal algorithms for k-search with application in option pricing. *Algorithmica*, 2009.
[3] E. Mohr, I. Ahmad, and G. Schmidt. Online algorithms for conversion problems: A survey. *Surveys in Operations Research and Management Science*, 19(2), 2014.
[4] L. Yang, M. H. Hajiesmaili, H. Yi, and M. Chen. Online offering strategies for storage-assisted renewable power producer in hour-ahead market. *arXiv preprint arXiv:1612.00179*, 2016.

Why "Some" Like It Hot Too: Thermal Attack on Data Centers

Xing Gao
University of Delaware
College of William and Mary
xgao@udel.edu

Zhang Xu
College of William and Mary
zxu@cs.wm.edu

Haining Wang
University of Delaware
hnw@udel.edu

Li Li
Ohio State University
Li.2251@osu.edu

Xiaorui Wang
Ohio State University
wang.3596@osu.edu

ABSTRACT

A trend in modern data centers is to raise the temperature and maintain all servers in a relatively hot environment. While this can save on cooling costs given benign workloads running in servers, the hot environment increases the risk of cooling failure. In this work, we introduce the security concept of thermal attack on a data center that exploits thermal-intensive workloads to severely worsen the thermal conditions in the data center. To unveil the vulnerability of a data center to thermal attacks, we conduct thermal measurements and propose effective thermal attack vectors. To evaluate the impacts of thermal attacks inside a data center, we simulate datacenter-level thermal attacks using a real-world data center trace. Our evaluation demonstrates that thermal attacks can cause local hotspots, and even worse lead to cooling failures.

ACM Reference format:
Xing Gao, Zhang Xu, Haining Wang, Li Li, and Xiaorui Wang. 2017. Why "Some" Like It Hot Too: Thermal Attack on Data Centers. In *Proceedings of SIGMETRICS '17, June 5–9, 2017, Urbana-Champaign, IL, USA, , 3 pages.*
DOI: http://dx.doi.org/10.1145/3078505.3078545

1   INTRODUCTION

The amount of heat emitted by today's data centers is surging, which requires the cooling system to more efficiently dissipate the increased heat. Otherwise, the overheating would potentially lead to serious hardware failures and even server shutdown for self-protection. To regulate the temperature in computer rooms, traditional CRAC (Computer Room Air Conditioning) cooling systems have been widely deployed in current data centers.

The key factor affecting the cooling cost of CRAC systems is the supply air temperature. A previous study shows that increasing the supply air temperature by merely 1°C can save approximately 2-5 percent of the cooling power [1]. Thus, there is a trend in data centers to raise the highest set temperature. Such an aggressive cooling energy saving policy forces the servers running in a hotter environment than before.

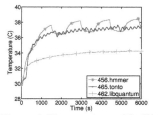 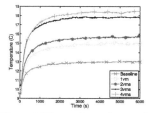

Figure 1: Temperature with different SPECCPU benchmarks.

Figure 2: Thermal attack on a virtualized environment.

Furthermore, advanced techniques like power oversubscripion have been widely adopted to accommodate more servers in data centers without upgrading existing power and cooling infrastructures. While the infrastructures were initially well designed with sufficient cooling redundancies, those redundancies have been excessively consumed as more powerful servers are deployed. In recent years, the online service interruptions due to cooling failures have not been rare in cloud vendors and enterprises.

In this work, we systematically investigate the security risk posed by those aggressive power and cooling policies applied on data centers. We introduce the concept of thermal attack, which can seriously worsen the thermal conditions at a server level, a rack level, or even a data center level. Thermal attacks simply run thermal-intensive workloads in victim servers to rapidly generate a large amount of heat. The accumulated heat can further exacerbate the thermal condition of the peripheral atmosphere, raising the inlet temperature of other servers. The consequence could be the thermal accidents that force some servers to shut down.

To form the basis for mounting a thermal attack, we first measure how thermal-related factors are exhibited in a real server using different High Performance Computing benchmarks. We observe that thermal-intensive workloads can generate more heat and cause a higher temperature than other types of workloads, even if the system utilization is at the same level. Then, we mount thermal attacks on a virtualized server. As expected, those attacks can largely raise the temperature of the hosting server within a short period time. Finally, we launch thermal attacks at the data center level using a CFD (computational fluid dynamics) based, trace-driven simulation, with a special consideration of the air recirculation condition in the data center. We observe that in some severe attack scenarios, thermal attacks can lead to cooling failures.

2   REAL SERVER MEASUREMENT

We perform a measurement study running in our small testbed. Our testbed is a mainstream Supermicro server, equipped with Intel

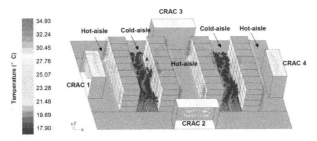

Figure 3: Layout of a typical data center.

Xeon 2.27GHz CPU with 16 cores, 32 GB of RAM. The testbed is placed in a sealed environment with the ambient temperature about 21°C cooled by the central air conditioner in our building.

We use a set of SPECCPU 2006 benchmarks to represent different types of workloads. We carefully choose these benchmarks, in which the system resources are consumed at the same level. To ensure exactly the same CPU utilization, we repeatedly and simultaneously run each benchmark with 16 copies to fully utilize all cores. Also, the memory consumptions of those benchmarks are similar. Figure 1 illustrates the outlet temperature of the testbed.

We observe that under the same system utilization, different types of workloads could lead to different thermal conditions. An almost 6°C temperature difference is generated by different workloads with the same CPU and memory utilization. 462.libquantum consumes a relatively high memory consumption but produces the minimum outlet temperature increment. By contrast, 456.hmmer can cause a much higher temperature increment than 462.libquantum, and 465.tonto raises the outlet temperature by more than 7°C while consuming the least amount of memory. The main reason could be that the types and ratios of instructions composing the benchmarks are different. Although the system utilization is the same, the underlying pipeline flows are actually very different. The ratio of different types of instructions, the probability of branch prediction, and the data dependence could be very different. Those differences further cause CPU halt and leave functional units idle, resulting in generating different amounts of heat.

3 THERMAL ATTACK

A simple approach to mounting a thermal attack is to rent a cloud instance and run thermal-intensive workloads in a VM (Virtual Machine), regardless of cloud service models, e.g., IaaS (Infrastructure as a Service). Recent research shows that it is still relatively easy to achieve tenant co-residence in public clouds. Once an attacker can run multiple VMs on the same physical machine, it can mount a more powerful thermal attack. Thus, the effective attack vector in a virtualized environment is to subscribe multiple VMs in one physical host and then run thermal-intensive workloads at the same time.

We emulate the IaaS services by running four VMs on our testbed, each VM allocated with 4GB memory and 4 cores, under the Xen hypervisor - the same type of hypervisors running in Amazon EC2. We run all VMs with 25% utilization as our baseline for representing a normal case. We then select one or more VM(s) with designed thermal-intensive workloads running to exhaust the host resources.

We measure the margin temperature (the difference between the outlet and inlet temperature) of the host when different numbers

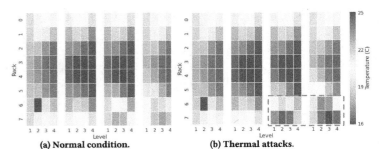

(a) Normal condition.   (b) Thermal attacks.

Figure 4: The global views of thermal conditions in a computer room.

of VMs run thermal-intensive workloads. The results in Figure 2 clearly demonstrate that with more VMs controlled, a thermal attack can heat the server to a higher temperature. Also, a thermal attack with three VMs involved can lead to about a 5°C higher temperature than the baseline case.

4 IMPACT ON DATA CENTERS

Thermal attacks greatly increase the surrounding environmental temperature of these victim servers, thus deteriorating the thermal conditions of the entire computer room. To evaluate the impact of thermal attacks at the data center level, we conduct a trace-driven simulation based on CFD, a powerful mechanical approach that can be used to simulate the air recirculation conditions.

For the data center layout, we use a standard layout with alternating hot and cold aisles, as illustrated in Figure 3. We assume that the targeted data center has one computer room, which contains four rows of servers, with eight racks in each row. Each rack contains 40 servers, totaling 1,280 servers. We use Fluent to simulate the thermal environment under different workload distributions, and then obtain the percentage of heat flow recirculated among the servers. We use a server trace file from one of the largest cloud service vendors, which contains the average CPU utilization of 5,415 servers in every 15 minutes for one week.

Figure 4 demonstrates the global views of thermal conditions in the targeted data center. Each block contains 10 servers and four blocks stack up as a rack. The level indicates the position of a block in a rack. The redline threshold for the inlet temperature is set to 25°C, representing the maximum temperature that servers could stay safe. The attacker first increases the utilization of controlled servers to the capping limit by running moderate workloads. Under this scenario as shown in Figure 4(a), the targeted data center still stays in a healthy thermal condition: the block with the highest temperature is about 22°C. After that, the attacker switches moderate workloads to thermal-intensive workloads at controlled servers. As Figure 4(b) shows, although all servers' utilizations remain unchanged, the thermal condition seriously deteriorates. The inlet temperature of multiple blocks at the right corner is approaching the redline threshold, and one of them already surpasses the redline temperature (25°C). Such results indicate that existing utilization-based load balance cannot defend against thermal attacks.

REFERENCES

[1] N. El-Sayed, I. A. Stefanovici, G. Amvrosiadis, A. A. Hwang, and B. Schroeder. Temperature management in data centers: why some (might) like it hot. *ACM SIGMETRICS*, 2012.

Incentivizing Reliable Demand Response with Customers' Uncertainties and Capacity Planning

Joshua Comden
Stony Brook University
joshua.comden@stonybrook.edu

Zhenhua Liu
Stony Brook University
zhenhua.liu@stonybrook.edu

Yue Zhao
Stony Brook University
yue.zhao.2@stonybrook.edu

ACM Reference format:
Joshua Comden, Zhenhua Liu, and Yue Zhao. 2017. Incentivizing Reliable Demand Response with Customers' Uncertainties and Capacity Planning. In *Proceedings of SIGMETRICS '17, June 5–9, 2017, Urbana-Champaign, IL, USA, ,* 2 pages.
DOI: http://dx.doi.org/10.1145/3078505.3078546

1 INTRODUCTION

One of the major issues with the integration of renewable energy sources into the power grid is the increased uncertainty and variability that they bring. If this uncertainty is not sufficiently addressed, it will limit the further penetration of renewables into the grid and even result in blackouts. Compared to energy storage, Demand Response (DR) has advantages to provide reserves to the load serving entities (LSEs) in a cost-effective and environmentally friendly way. DR programs work by changing customers' loads when the power grid experiences a contingency such as a mismatch between supply and demand. Uncertainties from both the customer-side and LSE-side make designing algorithms for DR a major challenge.

This paper makes the following main contributions: (i) We propose DR control policies based on the optimal structures of the offline solution. (ii) A distributed algorithm is developed for implementing the control policies without efficiency loss. (iii) We further offer an enhanced policy design by allowing flexibilities into the commitment level. (iv) We perform real world trace based numerical simulations which demonstrate that the proposed algorithms can achieve near optimal social cost. Details can be found in our extended version [3].

2 OPTIMIZATION PROBLEM

The goal is to *simultaneously* decide the capacity planning κ and a practical DR policy $\mathbf{x}(D, \delta)$ to minimize the *expected* social cost caused by a random aggregate supply-demand mismatch D (which captures mismatches from both the generation side and the load side).

$$\min_{\kappa, \mathbf{x}(D,\delta)} C_{\text{cap}}(\kappa)$$

$$+ \mathbb{E}_{D,\delta,C(\cdot)} \left[\sum_i C_i(x_i(D,\delta_i)) + C_g\left(D - \sum_i x_i(D,\delta_i)\right) \right]$$

$$\text{s.t.} \quad \max_{D,\delta} \left\{ D - \sum_i x_i(D,\delta_i) \right\} \leq \kappa \quad (1a)$$

$$\min_{D,\delta} \left\{ D - \sum_i x_i(D,\delta_i) \right\} \geq -\kappa. \quad (1b)$$

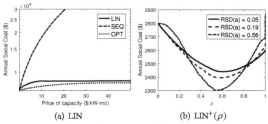

(a) LIN   (b) $\text{LIN}^+(\rho)$

Figure 1: Annual Social Cost vs. (a) price of capacity in LIN compared to different baselines, (b) level of commitment in $\text{LIN}^+(\rho)$ for different amounts of Relative Standard Deviations (RSD) on the customer cost parameter a.

where δ_i and $C_i(\cdot)$ are respectively for customer i the individual random demand mismatch and random cost function (e.g. $a_i x_i^2$ with a_i as a random coefficient) for performing DR, $C_{\text{cap}}(\cdot)$ and $C_g(\cdot)$ are respectively the LSE's cost for purchasing capacity and for managing the remaining mismatch, We note that (1a) and (1b) are worst-case constraints so that the remaining mismatch does not go beyond the purchased capacity. The two main challenges of this problem are (i) deciding the optimal capacity κ *before* implementing the DR policy, and (ii) optimizing an online DR policy. The cost functions are assumed to be convex.

Optimal Real-time Solution

We provide the characterization of the optimal real-time solution to reveal special structures that we take advantage of in our policy design (Section 3). The real-time DR decision problem for a given capacity κ at a time t is:

$$R(\kappa; t) := \min_{\mathbf{x}(t)} \quad \sum_i C_i(x_i(t); t) + C_g\left(D(t) - \sum_i x_i(t)\right) \quad (2a)$$

$$\text{s.t.} \quad -\kappa \leq D(t) - \sum_i x_i(t) \leq \kappa. \quad (2b)$$

LEMMA 2.1. *Problem (2) is a convex optimization problem.*

The Karush-Kuhn-Tucker (KKT) optimality conditions of this real-time problem show that when the capacity constraint on κ is non-binding, i.e., $-\kappa < D(t) - \sum_{j \in \mathcal{V}} x_j^*(t) < \kappa$, it implies that $C_i'(x_i^*(t)) = C_g'(D(t) - \sum_{j \in \mathcal{V}} x_j^*(t))$. This means that the marginal cost for each customer to provide demand response is the same, all of which is equal to the LSE's marginal cost to tolerate the mismatch. Furthermore, we get the following lemma which helps determine the optimal capacity in the next subsection:

LEMMA 2.2. $R(\kappa; t)$ *as defined by (2) is a convex function of κ. Additionally the negative of the sum of dual variables $\underline{\theta} + \overline{\theta}$ from constraint (2b) is the subgradient of $R(\kappa; t)$ w.r.t. κ.*

Optimal Capacity

We can use the real-time decision problem (2) to decide what the optimal capacity should be in the following capacity problem:

$$\min_{\kappa} \quad C_{\text{cap}}(\kappa) + \mathbb{E}_{D,\delta,C(\cdot)}[R(\kappa; t)] \quad (3)$$

THEOREM 2.3. (3) *is a convex optimization problem over* κ.

The KKT optimality conditions for the capacity problem and Lemma 2.2 give us the following result:

$$C'_{\text{cap}}(\kappa^*) = \mathbb{E}_{D,\delta,C(\cdot)}\left[\theta(\kappa^*;t)\right] \qquad (4)$$

where we use the notation of $\theta(\kappa;t)$ as a function to represent the sum of the optimal dual variables for constraint (2b). This means that for an optimal capacity, the marginal cost of capacity must equal the expected dual price for that capacity constraint.

3 POLICY DESIGN

Linear policy

Motivated by the desire to find a simple DR policy $\mathbf{x}(D, \delta_{i \in \mathcal{V}})$ that preserves convexity, we focus on a simple but powerful linear demand response policy that is a function of total and local net demands:

$$x_i(D, \delta_i) = \alpha_i D + \beta_i \delta_i + \gamma_i. \qquad (5)$$

Intuitively, there are three components: $\alpha_i D$ implies each customer shares some (predefined) fraction of the global mismatch D; $\beta_i \delta_i$ means customer i may need to take additional responsibility for the mismatch due to his own demand fluctuation and estimation error; finally, γ_i, the constant part, can help when the random variables $\mathbb{E}[D]$ and/or $\mathbb{E}[\delta_i]$ is nonzero. Then the LSE needs to solve (1) with (5) to obtain the optimal parameters for the linear contract, i.e., α, β, γ, as well as the optimal capacity κ.

THEOREM 3.1. *Problem* (1) *with the linear policy* (5) *is a convex optimization problem.*

Distributed algorithm

In most cases, the LSE's information on the customers' cost functions is much less accurate than the customer themselves'. This can also be due to privacy concerns. To handle this, we design a distributed algorithm so that the LSE does not need the information of the customer cost functions, while still achieving the optimal $(\kappa^{LIN}, \alpha^*, \beta^*, \gamma^*)$ for Problem (1) with the linear policy (5). We introduce and substitute (u_i, v_i, w_i) for $(\alpha_i, \beta_i, \gamma_i)$ in each customer's estimated cost function $\hat{C}_i(\cdot)$ and the LSE uses the corresponding price set $(\pi_i, \lambda_i, \mu_i)$ to incentivize each customer to change their parameters.

Distributed Algorithm for LIN:

(0) **Initialization:** $(\alpha, \beta, \gamma, \mathbf{u}, \mathbf{v}, \mathbf{w}, \pi, \lambda, \mu) := 0$.

(1) **LSE:** receives (u_i, v_i, w_i) from each customer $i \in \mathcal{V}$.
   - Solves Problem (9) and updates (α, β, γ) with the optimal solution.
   - Updates the stepsize:
   $$\eta = \frac{\zeta/k}{||(\alpha,\beta,\gamma)-(\mathbf{u},\mathbf{v},\mathbf{w})||_2} \qquad (6)$$
   where ζ is a small constant and k is the iteration number.
   - Updates the dual prices, $\forall i \in \mathcal{V}$:
   $(\pi_i, \lambda_i, \mu_i) := (\pi_i, \lambda_i, \mu_i) + \eta\left((\alpha_i, \beta_i, \gamma_i) - (u_i, v_i, w_i)\right)$ (7)
   - Sends $(\pi_i, \lambda_i, \mu_i)$ to the each customer respectively.

(2) **Customer** $i \in \mathcal{V}$: receives $(\pi_i, \lambda_i, \mu_i)$ from LSE.
   - Solves Problem (8) and updates (u_i, v_i, w_i) with optimal solution.
   - Sends (u_i, v_i, w_i) to the LSE.

(3) Repeat Steps 1-2 until $||(\alpha, \beta, \gamma) - (\mathbf{u}, \mathbf{v}, \mathbf{w})||_2 \leq \epsilon$ where ϵ is the tolerance on magnitude of the subgradient.

Thus $\pi_i u_i + \lambda_i v_i + \mu_i w_i$ is the total payment to customer i for the linear demand response policy. The individual customer's problem for a given set of prices is

$$\min_{u_i, v_i, w_i} \mathbb{E}_{D,\delta_i}\left[\hat{C}_i(u_i D + v_i \delta_i + w_i)\right] - \pi_i u_i - \lambda_i v_i - \mu_i w_i \qquad (8)$$

while the LSE's optimization problem among all the customers is

$$\min_{\alpha, \beta, \gamma, \kappa} \quad C_{\text{cap}}(\kappa) + \sum_{i \in \mathcal{V}}(\pi_i \alpha_i + \lambda_i \beta_i + \mu_i \gamma_i)$$
$$+ \mathbb{E}_{D,\delta}\left[C_g\left(\sum_{i \in \mathcal{V}}(\delta_i - \alpha_i D - \beta_i \delta_i - \gamma_i) - r\right)\right] \qquad (9)$$
$$\text{s.t. } (1a), (1b)$$

In order for the customers and the LSE to negotiate and obtain the optimal prices we use the Subgradient Method (see [2] Chapter 6).

THEOREM 3.2. *The distributed algorithm's trajectory of dual prices converge to the optimal dual prices for Problem* (1) *with* (5).

Flexible Commitment Demand Response

One potential drawback of LIN is that customers are forced to follow the specified linear policy. In some cases, customers may face a very high cost to follow the policy, e.g., when there are some critical jobs to be finished, represented by a larger $a_i(t)$. Motivated by this observation and some existing regulation service programs, we modify the LIN policy to add some flexibility limited by a single parameter ρ. We call the new algorithm $\text{LIN}^+(\rho)$ where each customer has up to $1 - \rho$ (in percentage) of the time slots in which they do not need to follow the policy according to her realized $a_i(t)$. In other words, she may let $x_i(t) = 0$ for such timeslots. Note that although we add the flexibility to LIN in this paper, the approach is in fact general and can be applied to a wide range of fully committed programs.

4 PERFORMANCE EVALUATION

Experimental Setup. We simulate an LSE supplying power to 300 customers. Each customer has a particular demand of load which we model by utilizing the traces obtained from the UMass Trace Repository [1].

LIN is close to optimal. Figure 1(a) compares the social cost of LIN to baselines using the offline optimal OPT (3) as a lower bound and sequential algorithm SEQ as an upper bound. The baseline SEQ first makes a conservative capacity planning decision about κ, and then sets a price for DR to obtain a targeted amount of DR. The social cost of LIN is no more than 10% higher compared to the fundamental limit OPT and is significantly less than SEQ. The social cost of SEQ increases rapidly with increasing capacity prices because of the conservative 90kW capacity used by SEQ to protect the system from *any* leftover mismatch.

Additional cost savings brought by $LIN^+(\rho)$. Depicted in Figure 1(b), as ρ decreases from 1, the social cost first decreases due to the fact that some customers with very high $a_i(t)$ are allowed to not provide demand response. As ρ continues to decrease, we have more customers not providing demand response and the cost actually goes up again. This is because the LSE's penalty for the mismatch becomes larger than the costs of customers to provide demand response. At $\rho = 0.8$, it achieves a cost savings 7-8%. Recall that the gap between LIN and the offline optimal OPT is about 10%. This means $\text{LIN}^+(\rho^*)$ achieves near optimal cost.

REFERENCES

[1] Sean Barker, Aditya Mishra, David Irwin, Emmanuel Cecchet, Prashant Shenoy, and Jeannie Albrecht. 2012. Smart*: An open data set and tools for enabling research in sustainable homes. *SustKDD, August* 111 (2012), 112.

[2] Dimitri P Bertsekas. 1999. *Nonlinear programming*. Athena scientific Belmont.

[3] Joshua Comden, Zhenhua Liu, and Yue Zhao. 2017. Incentivizing reliable demand response with customers' uncertainties and capacity planning. *arXiv preprint arXiv:1704.04537* (2017).

A Study on Performance and Power Efficiency of Dense Non-Volatile Caches in Multi-Core Systems

Amin Jadidi, Mohammad Arjomand, Mahmut Kandemir, and Chita Das
Pennsylvania State University

ABSTRACT

This paper presents a novel cache design based on *Multi-Level Cell Spin-Transfer Torque RAM* (MLC STT-RAM). Our design exploits the asymmetric nature of the MLC STT-RAM to build cache lines featuring heterogeneous performances, that is, half of the cache lines are read-friendly, while the other half are write-friendly – this asymmetry in read/write latencies are then used by a migration policy in order to overcome the high latency of the baseline MLC cache. Furthermore, in order to enhance the device lifetime, we propose to dynamically deactivate ways of a set in underutilized sets to convert MLC to *Single-Level Cell* (SLC) mode. Our experiments show that our design gives an average improvement of 12% in system performance and 26% in last-level cache (L3) access energy for various workloads.

ACM Reference format:
Amin Jadidi, Mohammad Arjomand, Mahmut Kandemir, and Chita Das. 2017. A Study on Performance and Power Efficiency of Dense Non-Volatile Caches in Multi-Core Systems. In *Proceedings of SIGMETRICS '17, June 5–9, 2017, Urbana-Champaign, IL, USA*, , 2 pages.
https://doi.org/http://dx.doi.org/10.1145/3078505.3078547

1 INTRODUCTION

STT-RAM has zero leakage power, accommodates almost 4× more density than SRAM, and has small read access latency and high endurance (compared to other non-volatile memories). Two types of STT-RAM cell prototypes can be realized: *Single-Level Cell (SLC)* STT-RAM and *Multi-Level Cell (MLC)* STT-RAM. The SLC STT-RAM cell consists of one storage component (MTJ) which is used to store one bit information. The MLC STT-RAM device is typically composed of multiple MTJs, which are connected either serially or in parallel, and are used to store more than one bit information in a single cell. Such increased density comes at the cost of linear increase in access latency and energy consumption. For instance, the read (or write) latency and energy consumption of a 2-bit STT-RAM cell is two times higher than that of a SLC STT-RAM device under same fabrication technology. Also, MLC STT-RAM usually has lower endurance (in terms of write cycles) than SLC.

In this paper, we propose a novel 2-bit MLC STT-RAM cache design to tackle the challenges brought by an MLC STT-RAM cache. We will discuss and experimentally show that our design achieves the best features of SLC and MLC STT-RAM configurations in a unified architecture.

2 THE PROPOSED MLC STT-RAM CACHE

Our design is mainly based on two policies: (i) the dynamic associativity policy, and (ii) the cache line swapping policy. The former tries to reduce unnecessary write traffic to the cache and hence improve its lifetime (as well as performance), while the latter tries to improve read and write access latencies. To achieve these goals, we use the stripped data-to-cell mapping, described below. A detailed description of our proposed cache design is available at [1].

2.1 Stripped Data-to-Cell Mapping

In a 2-bit MLC device, both bits are written or read together. We call this *stacked* data-to-cell mapping, in which the latency and energy consumption of the cache accesses are roughly twice as that of a SLC. An alternative way of storing data in an MLC cell is the *stripped* mapping, which basically exploits the read and write asymmetry of the two MTJs in MLC to build a fast read and fast write storage device. These two schemes are shown in Figure 1. In a read operation, the MSB can be read from the *hard-domain* in a single read cycle. On the other hand, the cost of writing into the *soft-domain* is lower. The *stripped* mapping groups the *hard-domains* together to form *Fast Read High-Energy write* (FRHE) lines, and groups the *soft-domains* to form *Slow Read Low-Energy write* (SRLE) lines. Figure 2 compares the memory access latency (seen by a missed data in L2 in our settings) for a 4MB stripped MLC cache compared to the same sized stacked cache and a 2MB SLC cache – that shows great amount of reduction in access latencies for all kinds of workloads.

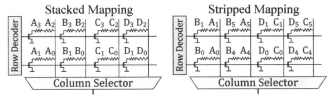

Figure 1: Stacked and stripped data-to-cell mapping..

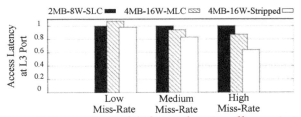

Figure 2: Comparison of different data-to-cell mappings.

2.2 The Need for Dynamic Associativity

Memory references in general purpose applications are often non-uniformly distributed across the sets of a set-associative cache,

SIGMETRICS '17, , June 5–9, 2017, Urbana-Champaign, IL, USA   Amin Jadidi, Mohammad Arjomand, Mahmut Kandemir, and Chita Das

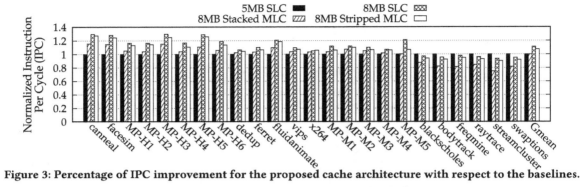

Figure 3: Percentage of IPC improvement for the proposed cache architecture with respect to the baselines.

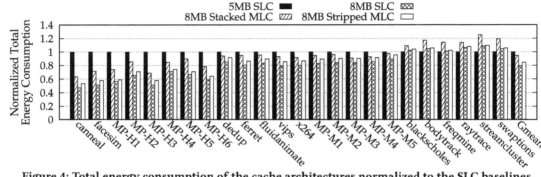

Figure 4: Total energy consumption of the cache architectures normalized to the SLC baselines.

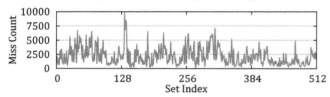

Figure 5: Distribution of the missed accesses in xalancbmk.

which can lead to a high number of local conflict misses in specific sets, while other sets are underutilized. This behavior is shown in Figure 5. Moreover, these opposite-behaving sets vary from one program phase to another. As a result, our proposed architecture involves an *on-demand associativity policy* which dynamically modulates the associativity of each set. To mitigate the effects of slow reads and high-energy writes, when a cache line needs to be turned off, an FRHE and SRLE pair is merged into an SLC line.

2.3   The Need for a Cache Line Swapping Policy

To further enhance our design, we propose a swapping policy to dynamically promote write-dominated data blocks to SRLE lines (i.e., low power write operations) and read-dominated ones to FRHE lines (i.e., fast read accesses).

3   EVALUATION RESULTS

Methodology: We perform a microarchitectural simulation using the Gem5 simulator. Each core also has private L1 and L2 caches. The STT-RAM L3 cache is shared among 8 cores. We also use PARSEC-2 and SPECCPU2006 (either in rate mode or multi-programmed mode).

Performance Evaluation: Figure 3 shows an improvement of up to 29% in IPC of the high associativity caches (i.e., MLC configurations and 8 MB SLC) with respect to the 5 MB SLC baseline. Our scheme also outperforms the 8 MB stacked 2-bit cache by 10% on average thanks to being able to construct FRHE and SRLE lines. Comparing the results with the 8 MB SLC shows that, the performance of our proposed cache structure is within 5% of the performance observed for the 8 MB SLC cache.

Energy Consumption: The percentage of reduction in total memory energy is shown in Figure 4. This evaluation includes the energy consumptions of both the LLC and off-chip main memory. The energy consumption of our proposed scheme is better than the SLC baseline in applications with high and medium miss-rates due to the higher hit ratio of LLC. Besides, the energy consumption of our scheme is better than the MLC baseline with the stacked data-to-cell mapping, as it constructs lines with low write energy and trying to allocate them write-dominated blocks.

Lifetime Evaluation: In this work, we assume that reliable writes into the SLC storage is limited to 10^{12} write operations, and it is linearly scaled down for 2-bit STT-RAMs (i.e., exactly one-tenth). Overall, our proposed scheme achieves a lifetime larger than 70% of lifetime of a 5 MB SLC cache, with identical ECC strength.

4   ACKNOWLEDGMENT

This work is supported in part by NSF grants 1302557, 1213052, 1439021, 1302225, 1629129, 1526750, and 1629915, a grant from Intel.

REFERENCES

[1] Amin Jadidi, Mohammad Arjomand, Mahmut T. Kandemir, and Chita R. Das. A Study on Performance and Power Efficiency of Dense Non-Volatile Caches in Multi-Core Systems, 2017. http://arxiv.org/abs/1704.05044

Scheduling Coflows in Datacenter Networks: Improved Bound for Total Weighted Completion Time

Mehrnoosh Shafiee and Javad Ghaderi
Department of Electrical Engineering
Columbia University

ABSTRACT

Coflow is a recently proposed networking abstraction to capture communication patterns in data-parallel computing frameworks. We consider the problem of efficiently scheduling coflows with release dates in a shared datacenter network so as to minimize the total weighted completion time of coflows. Specifically, we propose a randomized algorithm with approximation ratio of $3e \approx 8.155$, which improves the prior best known ratio of $9 + 16\sqrt{2}/3 \approx 16.542$. For the special case when all coflows are released at time zero, we obtain a randomized algorithm with approximation ratio of $2e \approx 5.436$ which improves the prior best known ratio of $3 + 2\sqrt{2} \approx 5.828$. Simulation result using a real traffic trace is presented that shows improvement over the prior approaches.

KEYWORDS

Scheduling Algorithms, Approximation Algorithms, Coflow, Datacenter Network

ACM Reference format:
Mehrnoosh Shafiee and Javad Ghaderi. 2017. Scheduling Coflows in Datacenter Networks: Improved Bound for Total Weighted Completion Time. In *Proceedings of SIGMETRICS '17, June 5–9, 2017, Urbana-Champaign, IL, USA, , 2 pages.*
DOI: http://dx.doi.org/10.1145/3078505.3078548

1 INTRODUCTION

Many data-parallel computing applications (e.g. MapReduce [3]) consist of multiple computation stages. Intermediate parallel data is often produced at various stages which needs to be transferred among servers in the datacenter network. A stage often cannot start or be completed unless all the required data pieces from the preceding stage are received. Hence, the collective effect of the data flflows between the stages is more important for the performance (e.g. latency, job completion time) than that of any of the individual flows. Recently Chowdhury and Stoica [1] have introduced the *coflow* abstraction to capture these communication patters. *A coflow is defined as a collection of parallel flows whose completion time is determined by the completion time of the last flow in the collection.* A Smallest-Effective-Bottleneck-First heuristic was introduced in Varys [2] for the problem of coflow scheduling in order to minimize the weighted sum of completion times of coflows in the system.

This work is supported by NSF Grants CNS-1652115 and CNS-1565774.

Table 1: Performance Guarantees (Approximation Ratios)

Case	Best known	This paper
Deterministic, without release dates	8 [5]	8
Deterministic, with release dates	12 [5]	12
Randomized, without release dates	$3 + 2\sqrt{2}$ [5]	$2e$
Randomized, with release dates	$9 + 16\sqrt{2}/3$ [6]	$3e$

This problem has been shown [5, 6] to be NP-complete through its connection with the concurrent open shop problem [2, 6]. Table 1 summarizes the best known approximation ratio results for this problem [5, 6]. We propose a deterministic algorithm that gives the same bound as the prior best known bound, however, our approach improves the best known bound for the randomized algorithm in both cases of with and without release dates.

2 MODEL AND PROBLEM STATEMENT

Similar to [2, 6], we abstract out the datacenter network as one giant $N \times N$ non-blocking switch, with N input and N output links connected to N source and N destination servers, respectively. We assume all the link capacities are equal and normalized to one. We assume there is a set of K coflows denoted by $\mathcal{K}$. Coflow $k \in \mathcal{K}$ can be denoted as an $N \times N$ matrix $D^{(k)}$ which is released at time r_k that means it can only be scheduled after time r_k. d_{ij}^k, the (i, j)-th element of the matrix $D^{(k)}$ is the size of flow (i, j, k). For a source node i and a coflow $k \in \mathcal{K}$, we define $d_i^k = \sum_{1 \le j \le N} d_{ij}^k$, which is the aggregate flow that node i needs to transmit for coflow k. d_j^k is defined similarly for destination node $j \in \mathcal{J}$ and coflow $k \in \mathcal{K}$. Moreover, $W(k) = \max\{\max_{1 \le i \le N} d_i^k, \max_{1 \le j \le N} d_j^k\}$ is defined as the effective size of coflow k.

We use f_k to denote the completion time of coflow k, which, by definition of coflow, is the time when all its flows have finished processing. In other words, for every coflow $k \in \mathcal{K}$, $f_k = \max_{1 \le i, j \le N} f_{ij}^k$, where f_{ij}^k is the completion time of flow (i, j, k).

For given positive weights w_k, $k \in \mathcal{K}$, the goal is to minimize the weighted sum of coflow completion times, i.e., $\sum_{k \in \mathcal{K}} w_k f_k$, subject to capacity and release dates constraints.

3 LINEAR PROGRAMING RELAXATION

In this section, we use *linear ordering variables* (see, e.g., [4]) to present a relaxed linear program of coflow scheduling problem. For any two coflows k, k', we introduce a binary variable $\delta_{kk'} \in \{0, 1\}$ such that $\delta_{kk'} = 1$ if coflow k is finished before coflow k', and it is 0 otherwise. In the linear program relaxation, we allow the ordering variables to be fractional. This yields the following relaxed LP

$$\text{(LP)} \quad \min \sum_{k=1}^{K} w_k f_k \tag{1a}$$

$$\text{subject to: } f_k \geq d_i^k + \sum_{k' \in \mathcal{K}} d_i^{k'} \delta_{k'k} \quad 1 \leq i \leq N, k \in \mathcal{K} \tag{1b}$$

$$f_k \geq d_j^k + \sum_{k' \in \mathcal{K}} d_j^{k'} \delta_{k'k} \quad 1 \leq j \leq N, k \in \mathcal{K} \tag{1c}$$

$$f_k \geq W(k) + r_k \quad k \in \mathcal{K} \tag{1d}$$

$$\delta_{kk'} + \delta_{k'k} = 1 \quad k, k' \in \mathcal{K} \tag{1e}$$

$$\delta_{kk'} \in [0, 1] \quad k, k' \in \mathcal{K}. \tag{1f}$$

The constraint (1b) (similarly (1c)) follows from the definition of ordering variables and the fact that flows incident to a source node i (a destination node j) are processed by a single link of unit capacity. The fact that each coflow cannot be completed before its release date plus its effective size is captured by constraint (1d). The next constraint (1e) indicates that for each two incident coflows, one precedes the other. We denote by $\tilde{f}_k$ the optimal solution to the (LP) for completion time of coflow $k \in \mathcal{K}$.

4 ALGORITHM DESCRIPTION AND MAIN RESULTS

Both deterministic and randomized algorithms have three steps: (i) solve the relaxed LP (1), (ii) use the solution of the relaxed LP to partition coflows into disjoint subsets $C_0, C_1, \cdots, C_L$ for some L to be determined, and (iii) treat each subset C_l, $l = 0, \cdots, L$, as a single coflow and schedule its flows in a way that optimizes its completion time.

Partition Rule: We define $\gamma = \min_{i,j,k} d_{ij}^k$ and $T = \max_k r_k + \sum_k \sum_i \sum_j d_{ij}^k$. Given $\beta \geq 1$ (to be optimized), we choose L to be the smallest integer such that $\gamma \beta^{L+\alpha} \geq T$, where in the deterministic algorithm, $\alpha = 0$ and in the randomized algorithm α is a number chosen uniformly at random from $[0, 1)$. Consequently, define $a_l = \gamma \beta^l$, for $l = -1, 0, 1, \cdots, L$. Then the l-th partition is defined as the interval $(a_{l-1}, a_l]$ in both algorithms and the set C_l is defined as the subset of coflows whose completion times $\tilde{f}_k$ fall within the l-th partition, i.e., $C_l = \{k \in \mathcal{K} : \tilde{f}_k \in (a_{l-1}, a_l]\}$; $l = 0, 1, \cdots, L$.

Scheduling Each Subset: To schedule coflows of each subset C_l, $l = 1, \cdots, L$, we construct a single coflow by aggregating all the coflows of C_l, and then schedule its flows to optimize the completion time of this aggregate coflow.

Suppose a single coflow $D = (d_{ij})_{i,j=1}^{N}$ is given. Let $W(D)$ denote its effective size. We assign transmission rate $x_{ij} = d_{ij}/W(D)$ to flow (i, j) until it is completed. Note that this rate assignment respects the capacity constraints, since for all source nodes $i \in \mathcal{I}$:

$$\sum_{1 \leq j \leq N} x_{ij}(t) = \sum_{1 \leq j \leq N} \frac{d_{ij}}{W(D)} \leq \frac{W(D)}{W(D)} = 1,$$

and similarly for all destination nodes $j \in \mathcal{J}$. Also, by this rate assignment, all flows of D finish in $W(D)$ amount of time.

Now we state the main results in the following theorems. Due to space constraint, we skip the proofs of these theorems and refer the reader to the technical report of this work [7].

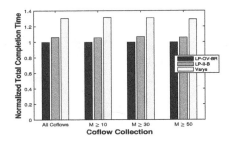

Figure 1: Performance of LP-OV-BR, LP-II-B, and Varys when all coflows release at time 0, normalized with the performance of LP-OV-BR, under real traffic trace.

THEOREM 4.1. *When $\beta = 2$, the described deterministic algorithm is a 12-approximation algorithm for the problem of total weighted completion time minimization of coflows with release dates. Without release dates, it is an 8-approximation algorithm.*

THEOREM 4.2. *When $\beta = e$, the described randomized algorithm is a $(3e)$-approximation algorithm. If all coflows are released at time 0, then it is a $(2e)$-approximation algorithm.*

5 EMPIRICAL EVALUATION

Now, we present our simulation result.

Workload: The workload is based on a Hive/MapReduce trace at Facebook that was collected from a 3000-machine cluster with 150 racks and was also used in [2, 6]. Similar to [6], we filter the coflows based on *the number of their non-zero flows which we denote by M.* Apart from considering all coflows ($M \geq 0$), we consider three coflow collections filtered by the conditions $M \geq 10$, $M \geq 30$, and $M \geq 50$. We assume that all coflows are released at time 0.

Algorithms: We combine backfilling strategy (see, e.g., [2, 6] with our algorithm and the algorithm in [6] and refer to them as 'LP-OV-BR' and 'LP-II-B', respectively. We also simulate Varys [2].

Figure 1 shows the performance of different algorithms for different collections of coflows when all coflows have equal weights. LP-OV-BR outperforms Varys by $28 - 32\%$ in different collections. It also constantly outperforms LP-II-B by $6 - 7\%$.

More simulation results are presented in the technical report [7].

REFERENCES
[1] Mosharaf Chowdhury and Ion Stoica. 2012. Coflow: A networking abstraction for cluster applications. In *Proceedings of the 11th ACM Workshop on Hot Topics in Networks.* ACM, 31–36.
[2] Mosharaf Chowdhury, Yuan Zhong, and Ion Stoica. 2014. Efficient coflow scheduling with Varys. In *ACM SIGCOMM Computer Communication Review,* Vol. 44. ACM, 443–454.
[3] Jeffrey Dean and Sanjay Ghemawat. 2008. MapReduce: simplified data processing on large clusters. *Commun. ACM* 51, 1 (2008), 107–113.
[4] Rajiv Gandhi, Magnús M Halldórsson, Guy Kortsarz, and Hadas Shachnai. 2008. Improved bounds for scheduling conflicting jobs with minsum criteria. *ACM Transactions on Algorithms (TALG)* 4, 1 (2008), 11.
[5] Samir Khuller and Manish Purohit. 2016. Brief Announcement: Improved Approximation Algorithms for Scheduling Co-Flows. In *Proceedings of the 28th ACM Symposium on Parallelism in Algorithms and Architectures.* ACM, 239–240.
[6] Zhen Qiu, Cliff Stein, and Yuan Zhong. 2015. Minimizing the total weighted completion time of coflows in datacenter networks. In *Proceedings of the 27th ACM symposium on Parallelism in Algorithms and Architectures.* ACM, 294–303.
[7] Mehrnoosh Shafiee and Javad Ghaderi. 2017. *Scheduling Coflows in Datacenter Networks: Improved Bound for Total Weighted Completion Time.* Technical Report. http://www.columbia.edu/~ms4895/technical%20report/coflowsig.pdf.

Characterizing 3D Floating Gate NAND Flash

Qin Xiong[†], Fei Wu[†], Zhonghai Lu[‡], Yue Zhu[†], You Zhou[†], Yibing Chu[§], Changsheng Xie[†], Ping Huang[¶]

[†]Wuhan National Laboratory for Optoelectronics, Huazhong University of Science and Technology, Wuhan, China
[‡]School of Information and Communication Technology, KTH Royal Institute of Technology, Stockholm, Sweden
[§]Renice Technology Co. Limited, China   [¶]Department of Computer Information Sciences, Temple University, USA
qinxiong@kth.se, wufei@hust.edu.cn, zhonghai@kth.se, {yuezhu, zhouyou}@hust.edu.cn
eric@renice-tech.com, Cs_xie@hust.edu.cn, templestorager@temple.edu

ABSTRACT

In this paper, we characterize a state-of-the-art 3D floating gate NAND flash memory through comprehensive experiments on an FPGA platform. Then, we present distinct observations on performance and reliability, such as operation latencies and various error patterns. We believe that through our work, novel 3D NAND flash-oriented designs can be developed to achieve better performance and reliability.

1 INTRODUCTION

NAND flash memory has been widely used as a popular storage medium in different systems. However, when the feature size decreases to be less than 30 nm, flash scaling becomes particularly challenging because of the technical complexity, the decreasing electrons that can be retained by a cell [2], and the dramatically rising cell-to-cell interferences.

3D NAND flash architecture represents a promising opportunity to overcome the limitations of planar devices since it allows flash storage to continue aligning with Moore's Law while expected to provide higher reliability. Currently, there are two types of NAND flash cells in industry, *floating gate* (FG) and *charge trap* (CT) [3]. The main difference between them is that an FG cell uses a floating gate made of doped polycrystalline silicon to store electrons rather than a silicon nitride film of a CT structure. In this paper, our research focuses on 3D FG NAND flash, and we expect the studying of 3D CT NAND flash as an important area of future work. *In the rest of this paper, unless otherwise stated, we use 3D NAND flash to refer to 3D FG NAND flash for simplicity.*

Flash exhibits unique physical features and error patterns from spinning disks, thus several management techniques, e.g., *Page mapping* [4], *Garbage collection (GC)*, *Error correction codes (ECCs)*, *Wear leveling* and *Bad block management*, are necessary to build a flash-based storage system. Since these techniques are closely related to the characteristics of underlying flash [1], it is critical and urgent to have a strong understanding about the characteristics of 3D NAND flash.

Corresponding Author: Fei Wu, wufei@hust.edu.cn

To the best of our knowledge, this is the first paper to empirically analyze characteristics of 3D NAND flash. In this paper, we conduct extensive experimental evaluations on 32-tier 3D MLC NAND flash chips, perform a comprehensive data analysis and discuss the implications of our observations.

2 EVALUATION

Evaluation Setup. We have built an FPGA-based NAND flash testing platform that gives us the abilities to directly control the pins of devices, and use a high-low temperature test chamber to accelerate retention error tests. For our experiments, we choose the state-of-the-art Intel-Micron 32-tier 3D MLC NAND flash chips manufactured in 2016. In these chips, the 2 top-most and 2 bottom-most tiers work in SLC mode, and the 30 middle tiers are in MLC mode, with each tier containing 16 wordlines (WLs).

Observation 1. Erase and program latencies of SLC pages and upper pages in MLC mode vary predictably as P/E cycle increases, and program latency among tiers varies greatly, as shown in Fig. 1. The first phenomenon is caused by the intrinsic property of FG cells, accumulating more defects on the tunnel oxide as P/E cycle increases, and the second is due to the *cross-tier process variations*.

Observation 2. In 3D NAND flash, the endurance of blocks is fluctuant in a chip and falls down significantly compared with planar NAND flash, and pages in a block exhibit different degradation speeds and the speeds accelerate dramatically with P/E cycles, as shown in Fig. 2 and 3. This is because as an alternative solution in the 3D era, the first-generation products of 3D NAND flash have not been released until 2015, and the process control and the quality among pages are imperfect and unstable compared with planar flash, which has been researched and produced for decades.

Observation 3. Different WLs in the vertical direction make different contributions to program disturb errors, while WLs introduce similar levels of program disturbs to the other WLs in the same tier, as shown in Fig. 4. These phenomena are due to the two main factors for program disturb among tiers and among WLs within a tier are parasitic capacitance coupling effects, which decreases dramatically with the distance, and high control gate voltages, the same level of which WLs within a tier suffer, respectively.

Observation 4. The neighboring tiers of a target page suffer much more serious read disturbs than other tiers, as shown in Fig. 5. The reason of higher read disturb errors in adjacent tiers is that higher level of pass voltage is actually

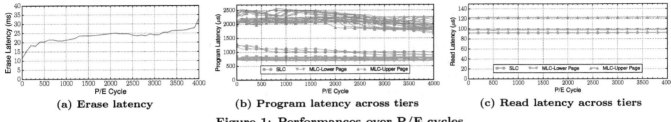

(a) Erase latency   (b) Program latency across tiers   (c) Read latency across tiers

Figure 1: Performances over P/E cycles.

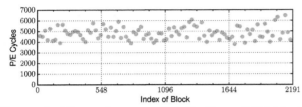

Figure 2: The endurance distribution of 100 blocks.

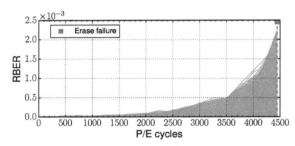

Figure 3: Degradation speed variations among pages.

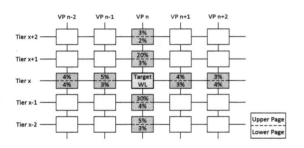

Figure 4: Normalized contributions of two adjacent WLs in horizontal and vertical directions to program disturb errors.

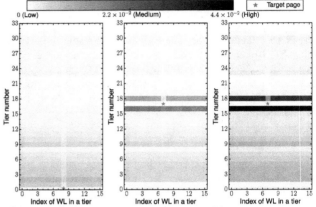

(a) Read SLC page (b) Read lower page (c) Read upper page

Figure 5: Distributions of read disturb errors among WLs in a block after 2 million read operations under the wear of 4000 P/E cycles.

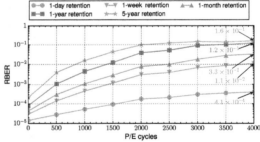

Figure 6: RBERs vs. P/E cycles with various retention ages.

applied to these tiers to reduce the coupling effect, introducing a stronger *weak programming effect*.

Observation 5. Raw bit error rates (RBERs) rise rapidly with retention ages and P/E cycles, and reach very high levels after 1-week retention or longer, as shown in Fig. 6.

For these observations, some characteristic-based policies, such as write heterogeneity-aware page allocation policy, erase suspend and resume in GC, rate-adaptive ECC, latency-based bad block predictions and read disturb-aware refresh policy, can be used to manage 3D floating gate NAND flash more efficiently and reliably.

ACKNOWLEDGMENTS

This research is sponsored by the National Natural Science Foundation of China under Grant No. 61300047, No. 61472152 and No. 61572209, the Fundamental Research Funds for the Central Universities No. 2016YXMS019, the 111 Project No. B07038, and the Key Laboratory of Data Storage System, Ministry of Education of China.

REFERENCES

[1] Peter Desnoyers. 2013. What systems researchers need to know about NAND flash. In *Proc. of HotStorage*. USENIX, 1–5.
[2] Kinam Kim. 2008. Future memory technology: Challenges and opportunities. In *Proc. of VLSI-TSA*. IEEE, 5–9.
[3] Rino Micheloni. 2016. *3D Flash Memories*. Springer.
[4] You Zhou, Fei Wu, and Ping Huang, et al. 2015. An efficient page-level FTL to optimize address translation in flash memory. In *Proc. of EuroSys*. ACM, 1–16.

ECF: An MPTCP Path Scheduler to Manage Heterogeneous Paths

Yeon-sup Lim
University of Massachusetts Amherst
ylim@cs.umass.edu

Erich M. Nahum
IBM Research
nahum@us.ibm.com

Don Towsley
University of Massachusetts Amherst
towsley@cs.umass.edu

Richard J. Gibbens
University of Cambridge
richard.gibbens@cl.cam.ac.uk

ABSTRACT

Multi-Path TCP (MPTCP) is a new standardized transport protocol that enables devices to utilize multiple network interfaces. The default MPTCP path scheduler prioritizes paths with the smallest round trip time (RTT). In this work, we examine whether the default MPTCP path scheduler can provide applications the ideal aggregate bandwidth, i.e., the sum of available bandwidths of all paths. Our experimental results show that heterogeneous paths cause under-utilization of the fast path, resulting in undesirable application behaviors such as lower video streaming quality than can be obtained using the available aggregate bandwidth. To solve this problem, we propose and implement a new MPTCP path scheduler, ECF (Earliest Completion First), that utilizes all relevant information about a path, not just RTT. Our results show that ECF consistently utilizes all available paths more efficiently than other approaches under path heterogeneity, particularly for streaming video.

CCS CONCEPTS

• **Networks** → *Transport protocols*; *Network experimentation*;

1 INTRODUCTION

One significant factor that affects MPTCP performance is the design of the path scheduler, which distributes traffic across available paths according to a particular scheduling policy. The default path scheduler of MPTCP is based on round trip time (RTT) estimates, that is, given two paths with available congestion window space, it prefers to send traffic over the path with the smallest RTT. While simple and intuitive, this scheduling policy does not carefully consider path heterogeneity, where available bandwidths and round trip times of the two paths differ considerably. This *path heterogeneity* is common in mobile devices with multiple interfaces [2, 4, 5, 9, 12] and can cause significant reorderings at the receiver-side [1–3, 7, 13]. To prevent this, MPTCP includes opportunistic retransmission and penalization mechanisms along with the default scheduler [10]. In long-lived flows, e.g., large file transfer, MPTCP is able to enhance performance using these mechanisms. However, a large number of Internet applications such as Web browsing and video streaming usually generate traffic which consists of multiple

SIGMETRICS '17, June 5–9, 2017, Urbana-Champaign, IL, USA

© 2017 Copyright held by the owner/author(s). ACM ISBN 978-1-4503-5032-7/17/06.

DOI: http://dx.doi.org/10.1145/3078505.3078552

uploads/downloads for relatively short durations. We find that in the presence of path heterogeneity, the default MPTCP scheduler is unable to efficiently utilize some paths with such a traffic pattern. In particular it does not fully utilize the highest bandwidth paths, which should be prioritized to achieve the highest performance and lowest response time.

In this work, we propose a novel MPTCP path scheduler to maximize fast path utilization, called ECF (Earliest Completion First). To this end, ECF monitors not only RTT estimates, but also the current subflow bandwidths (i.e., congestion windows) and the amount of data available to send (i.e., the send buffer). By determining whether using a slow path for the injected traffic will cause faster paths to become idle, ECF more efficiently utilizes the faster paths, maximizing throughput, minimizing download time, and reducing out-of-order packet delivery. Our experimental results demonstrate that ECF successfully avoids undesirable idle periods, achieving greater throughput with higher path utilization than the default scheduler. At the same time, it performs as well as other schedulers under homogeneous path conditions.

2 THE EFFECT OF PATH HETEROGENEITY

We examine the effect of path heterogeneity on application performance using adaptive video streaming, since it is currently one of the dominant applications in use over the Internet [11]. We measure the average video bit rate obtained by an Android DASH (Dynamic Adaptive Streaming over HTTP) streaming client while limiting the bandwidth of the WiFi and LTE subflows on the server-side using the Linux traffic control utility tc [8]. The streaming client uses a state-of-art adaptive bit rate selection (ABR) algorithm [6]. The choice of ABR does not significantly affect the results in this experiment as we use fixed bandwidths for each interface. The opportunistic retransmission and penalization mechanisms are enabled by default. Each experiment consists of five runs, where a run consists of the playout of the 20 minute video of which available resolutions are 144p to 1080p. Table 1 presents the bit rates corresponding to each resolution. We choose bandwidth amounts slightly larger than those listed in Table 1, i.e., $\{0.3, 0.7, 1.1, 1.7, 4.2, 8.6\}$ Mbps, to ensure there is sufficient bandwidth for that video encoding.

Figure 1(a) presents the ratio of the average bit rate achieved versus the ideal average bit rate available, based on the bandwidth combinations, when using the default MPTCP path scheduler. The figure is a grey-scale heat map where the darker the area is, the closer to the ideal bit rate the streaming client experiences. The closer the ratio is to one, the better the scheduler does in achieving the potential available bandwidth. The values are averaged over

Resolution	144p	240p	360p	480p	760p	1080p
Bit Rate (Mbps)	0.26	0.64	1.00	1.60	4.14	8.47

Table 1: Video Bit Rates vs. Resolution

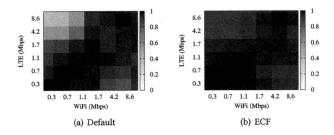

(a) Default   (b) ECF

Figure 1: Ratio of Measured Average Bit Rate vs. Ideal Average Bit Rate (darker is better)

five runs. In a streaming workload, we define the ideal average bit rate as the minimum of the aggregate total bandwidth and the bandwidth required for the highest resolution at that bandwidth. For example, in the 8.6 Mbps WiFi and 8.6 Mbps LTE pair (the upper right corner in Figure 1(a)), the ideal average bit rate is 8.47 Mbps, since the ideal aggregate bandwidth (8.6 + 8.6 = 17.2 Mbps) is larger than the required bandwidth for the highest resolution of 1080p (8.47 Mbps). Since the full bit rate is achieved, the value is one and the square is black.

Figure 1(a) shows that, when significant path heterogeneity exists, the streaming client fails to obtain the ideal bit rate. For example, when WiFi and LTE provide 0.3 Mbps and 8.6 Mbps, respectively (the upper left box in Figure 1), the streaming client retrieves 480p video chunks, which requires only 2 Mbps, even though the ideal aggregate bandwidth is larger than 8.47 Mbps. Thus, the value is only 25% of the ideal bandwidth and the square is light grey. This problem becomes even more severe when the primary path (WiFi) becomes slower (compare the 0.3 Mbps & [0.3 – 8.6] Mbps and 8.6 Mbps & [0.3 – 8.6Mbps] pairs), as shown by the grey areas in the upper left and lower right corners.

3 ECF SCHEDULER

To solve the performance degradation problem with path heterogeneity, we propose a new MPTCP path scheduler, called ECF (Earliest Completion First). An MPTCP sender stores packets both in its connection-level send buffer and in the subflow level send buffer (if the packet is assigned to that subflow). Assume that there are k packets in the connection level send buffer, which have not been assigned (scheduled) to any subflow. If the fastest subflow in terms of RTT has available CWND, the packet can simply be scheduled to that subflow. If the fastest subflow does not have available space, the packet needs to be scheduled to the second fastest subflow.

We denote the fastest and the second fastest subflows as x_f and x_s, respectively. Let RTT_f, RTT_s and $CWND_f$, $CWND_s$ be the RTTs and CWNDs of x_f and x_s, respectively. If the sender waits until x_f becomes available and then transfers k packets through x_f, it will take approximately $RTT_f + \frac{k}{CWND_f} \times RTT_f$, i.e., the waiting

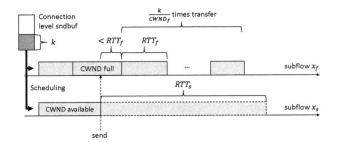

Figure 2: The case for waiting for the fast subflow

and transmission time of k packets. Otherwise, if the sender sends some packets over x_s, the transmission will finish after RTT_s with or without completing k packet transfers. Thus, as shown in Figure 2, in the case of $RTT_f + \frac{k}{CWND_f} \times RTT_f < RTT_s$, using x_f after it becomes available can complete the transmission earlier than using x_s immediately. If $RTT_f + \frac{k}{CWND_f} \times RTT_f \geq RTT_s$, there are sufficient number of packets to send, so that using x_s at that moment can decrease the transmission time by utilizing more bandwidth than just by using x_f.

ECF checks the above inequality to decide whether it will wait for x_f or immediately use x_s. Figure 1(b) shows that ECF successfully enables the streaming client to obtain average bit rates closest to the ideal average bit rate, and does substantially better than the default when paths are homogeneous.

REFERENCES

[1] Y.-C. Chen, Y.-S. Lim, R. J. Gibbens, E. Nahum, R. Khalili, and D. Towsley. A measurement-based study of Multipath TCP performance in wireless networks. In *Proc. of ACM IMC*, pages 455–468, Nov 2013.

[2] S. Deng, R. Netravali, A. Sivaraman, and H. Balakrishnan. WiFi, LTE, or both? Measuring multi-homed wireless Internet performance. In *Proc. of ACM IMC*, 2014.

[3] S. Ferlin, O. Alay, O. Mehani, and R. Boreli. BLEST: Blocking estimation-based MPTCP scheduler for heterogeneous networks. In *Proc. of IFIP Networking*, pages 1222–1227, 2016.

[4] B. Han, F. Qian, L. Ji, and V. Gopalakrishnan. MP-DASH: Adaptive video streaming over preference-aware multipath. In *Proc. of ACM CoNEXT*, 2016.

[5] J. Huang, Q. Feng, A. Gerber, Z. M. Mao, S. Sen, and O. Spatscheck. A close examination of performance and power characteristics of 4G LTE networks. In *Proc. of ACM MobiSys*, pages 225–238, 2012.

[6] T.-Y. Huang, R. Johari, N. McKeown, M. Trunnell, and M. Watson. A buffer-based approach to rate adaptation: Evidence from a large video streaming service. In *Proc. of ACM SIGCOMM*, pages 187–198, 2014.

[7] N. Kuhn, E. Lochin, A. Mifdaoui, G. Sarwar, O. Mehani, and R. Boreli. DAPS: Intelligent delay-aware packet scheduling for multipath transport. In *Proc. of IEEE ICC*, pages 1222–1227, 2014.

[8] Linux Foundation. Linux advanced routing and traffic control. http://lartc.org/howto/.

[9] A. Nikravesh, Y. Goo, F. Qian, Z. M. Mao, and S. Sen. An in-depth understanding of multipath TCP on mobile devices: Measurement and system design. In *Proc. of ACM MobiCom*, 2016.

[10] C. Raiciu, C. Paasch, S. Barre, A. Ford, M. Honda, F. Duchene, O. Bonaventure, and M. Handley. How hard can it be? Designing and implementing a deployable multipath TCP. In *Proc. of USENIX NSDI*, pages 399–412, 2012.

[11] Sandvine. Global Internet phenomena report, Latin America and North America 2016. https://www.sandvine.com/downloads/general/global-internet-phenomena/2016/global-internet-phenomena-report-latin-america-and-north-america.pdf.

[12] J. Sommers and P. Barford. Cell vs. wifi: on the performance of metro area mobile connections. In *Proceedings of the 2012 ACM conference on Internet measurement conference*, pages 301–314. ACM, 2012.

[13] F. Yang, P. Amer, and N. Ekiz. A scheduler for multipath TCP. In *Proc. of ICCCN*, pages 1–7, 2013.

Simplex Queues for Hot-Data Download

Mehmet Fatih Aktaş
Rutgers University
mehmet.aktas@rutgers.edu

Elie Najm
EPFL Lausanne
elie.najm@epfl.ch

Emina Soljanin
Rutgers University
emina.soljanin@rutgers.edu

CCS CONCEPTS

•**Mathematics of computing** → **Queueing theory; Renewal theory; Markov processes;**

KEYWORDS

Queues with Redundancy; Availability; Locally Repairable Codes

ACM Reference format:
Mehmet Fatih Aktaş, Elie Najm, and Emina Soljanin. 2017. Simplex Queues for Hot-Data Download. In *Proceedings of SIGMETRICS '17, June 5–9, 2017, Urbana-Champaign, IL, USA, ,* 2 pages.
DOI: http://dx.doi.org/10.1145/3078505.3078553

1   INTRODUCTION AND SYSTEM MODEL

In distributed systems, reliable data storage is accomplished through redundancy, which has traditionally been achieved by simple replication of data across multiple nodes [6]. A special class of erasure codes, known as locally repairable codes (LRCs) [7], has started to replace replication in practice [8], as a more storage-efficient way to provide a desired reliability. It has recently been recognized, that storage redundancy can also provide fast access of stored data (see e.g. [5, 9, 10] and references therein). Most of these papers consider download scenarios of all jointly encoded pieces of data, and very few [11, 12, 14] are concerned with download of only some, possibly hot, pieces of data that are jointly encoded with those of less interest. So far, only low traffic regime has been partially addressed.

In this paper, we are concerned with hot data download from systems implementing a special class of locally repairable codes, known as LRCs with availability [13, 15]. We consider simplex codes, a particular subclass of LRCs with availability, because 1) they are in a certain sense optimal [2] and 2) they are minimally different from replication. In a distributed system implementing a simplex code, a particular piece of data can be downloaded either from a single, *systematic*, node storing this piece or from any of the t pairs of nodes, *repair groups*, where this piece of data is encoded jointly with others, see Fig. 1. The number of repair groups that can disjointly serve a piece of data is called the code *availability t*, and the size of the repair group is called the code *locality r*.

Therefore, a data download request can be served exclusively by the systematic node or by any of the repair groups, or redundantly by some subset of these options. We consider two data download request scheduling strategies: 1) *Replicate-to-all* where requests are simultaneously directed to the systematic and all repair groups and 2) *Select-one* where requests are forwarded to either the systematic

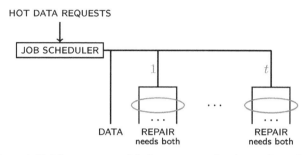

Figure 1: Hot data access models from a system implementing a simplex code. In *replicate-to-all,* **the job scheduler dispatches the request to the systematic node containing data and to all its repair groups. In** *select-one,* **the job scheduler randomly choses either the systematic node or one of the repair groups. One can consider other access schemes between these two polarities.**

node or one of the repair groups at a time. The low-traffic regime analysis for these scheduling strategies was considered in [11, 12] for general LRCs with availability. When the low-traffic assumption does not hold, download time analysis for the replicate-to-all strategy involves analyzing multiple, inter-dependent, fork-join type queues. We next state several results and refer the reader to [1] for proofs and other contributions.

2   RESULTS AND CONTRIBUTIONS

We assume Poisson request arrivals at rate rate λ, and $Exp(\mu)$ service time, iid across nodes. A more realistic service time model, proposed recently in [4] for systems with redundancy, will be considered in further extensions of this work.

State space of the system, which we refer to as Simplex(t), under replicate-to-all scheduling is very complex. Download requests are replicated, and immediately upon the completion of any replica, all others are removed. Replicas sent to a repair group are forked to two queues and joined when they complete. These inter-dependent fork-join queues make the exact analysis formidable given that analysis of fork-join queues itself is a notoriously hard problem, even when the number of queues is two [3]. We next present a framework to approximate the average download time (cf. Thm. 2.2).

We define the service start time of a request as the epoch at which the last batch of its $t + 1$ replicas enters service. We distinguish $t + 1$ types of possible service starts as follows. Type-j service start, $j = 0, \ldots, t$, means that at exactly j repair groups, one forked copy completed service before the request starts service, that is, before the remaining of the $t + 1 - j$ replicas enter service. Each type of service start dictates a different service time distribution. Requests depart the system in the order they arrive but service time distributions of subsequent requests are dependent. However they are only loosely coupled, and the system experiences frequent renewal epochs, between which the service times are independent.

This observation, which is also validated by the simulations, lead us to approximate the system as an M/G/1 queue.

LEMMA 2.1. *Under replicate-to-all scheduling in Simplex(t), an arbitrary download request has one of the service time distribution V_j's for $j = 0, \ldots, t$ with moments*

$$E[V_i] = \sum_{k=0}^{t-i} \binom{t-i}{k} 2^k (-1)^{t-i-k} \frac{1}{\mu(2t+1-i-k)},$$

$$E[V_i^2] = \sum_{k=0}^{t-i} \binom{t-i}{k} 2^k (-1)^{t-i-k} \frac{2}{(\mu(2t+1-i-k))^2}. \tag{1}$$

THEOREM 2.2. *Under replicate-to-all scheduling, Simplex(t) can be approximated as an M/G/1 queue and the Pollaczek-Khinchin formula approximates the average download time as*

$$E[T] \approx E[V] + \frac{\lambda E[V^2]}{2(1 - \lambda E[V])} \tag{2}$$

where moments of service time V are given by

$$E[V] = \sum_{j=0}^{t} f_j E[V_j], \qquad E[V^2] = \sum_{j=0}^{t} f_j E[V_j^2]. \tag{3}$$

where f_j is the probability that an arbitrary request has service time distribution V_j with moments given in (1).

Even though exact analysis is formidable, we find estimates of the probabilities for service time distributions (f_j's in Theorem 2.2) by analyzing system under "high-traffic", where system is assumed to be always busy. Specifically, for the simplest simplex code with availability $t = 1$, high-traffic assumption reduces the state space to a birth death Markov chain, the analysis of which gives good estimates of f_j's. Unfortunately this approach quickly becomes intractable for higher availability. However, we conjecture that f_j's are related as $f_0 \geq f_1 \geq \ldots \geq f_t$. Using this hypothesis and the fact that system experiences frequent renewals, we obtain good estimates of f_j's. Fig. 2 shows the resulting approximations for average download time using these estimates.

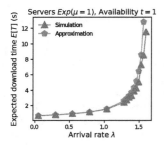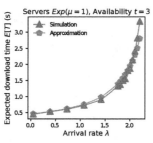

Figure 2: Comparison of the approximations and the simulated average download time $E[T]$ for Simplex(t) under replicate-to-all scheduling where $t = 1$ (Left) and $t = 3$ (Right).

Under select-one scheduling, the system is simpler to analyze, and we can get exact expression of the expected download time.

THEOREM 2.3. *Under select-one scheduling in Simplex(t) with the probability p_i of forwarding a request independently to repair group*

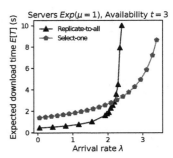

Figure 3: Comparison of the average download time with replicate-to-all and select-one for Simplex($t = 3$).

i for $i = 0, \ldots, t$, the average download time is

$$E[T] = \frac{p_0}{\gamma - p_0 \lambda} + \sum_{i=1}^{t} p_i \frac{12\mu - p_i \lambda}{8\mu(\mu - p_i \lambda)} \tag{4}$$

Note that under low arrival rate replicate-to-all achieves lower download time by exploiting redundancy aggressively while select-one achieves higher scalability by load balancing i.e., can achieve stability for higher arrival rates (Fig. 3). An important feature of availability codes is that they allow system to switch between these two scheduling strategies without having to recode data.

REFERENCES

[1] Mehmet Aktas, Elie Najm, and Emina Soljanin. 2017. *Simplex Queues for Hot-Data Download.* Technical Report.
[2] Viveck R. Cadambe and Arya Mazumdar. 2015. Bounds on the Size of Locally Recoverable Codes. *IEEE Trans. Information Theory* 61, 11 (2015), 5787–5794.
[3] Leopold Flatto and S Hahn. 1984. Two parallel queues created by arrivals with two demands I. *SIAM J. Appl. Math.* 44, 5 (1984), 1041–1053.
[4] Kristen Gardner, Mor Harchol-Balter, and Alan Scheller-Wolf. 2016. A better model for job redundancy: Decoupling server slowdown and job size. In *Modeling, Analysis and Simulation of Computer and Telecommunication Systems (MASCOTS), 2016 IEEE 24th International Symposium on.* IEEE, 1–10.
[5] Kristen Gardner, Samuel Zbarsky, Sherwin Doroudi, Mor Harchol-Balter, and Esa Hyytia. 2015. Reducing latency via redundant requests: Exact analysis. *ACM SIGMETRICS Performance Evaluation Review* 43, 1 (2015), 347–360.
[6] Sanjay Ghemawat, Howard Gobioff, and Shun-Tak Leung. 2003. The Google file system. In *ACM SIGOPS operating systems review,* Vol. 37. ACM, 29–43.
[7] Parikshit Gopalan, Cheng Huang, Huseyin Simitci, and Sergey Yekhanin. 2012. On the locality of codeword symbols. *IEEE Transactions on Information Theory* 58, 11 (2012), 6925–6934.
[8] Cheng Huang, Huseyin Simitci, Yikang Xu, Aaron Ogus, Brad Calder, Parikshit Gopalan, Jin Li, and Sergey Yekhanin. 2012. Erasure coding in windows azure storage. In *Presented as part of the 2012 USENIX Annual Technical Conference (USENIX ATC 12).* 15–26.
[9] Gauri Joshi, Yanpei Liu, and Emina Soljanin. 2014. On the Delay-Storage Trade-Off in Content Download from Coded Distributed Storage Systems. *IEEE Journal on Selected Areas in Communications* 32, 5 (2014), 989–997.
[10] Gauri Joshi, Emina Soljanin, and Gregory W. Wornell. to appear, 2017. Efficient Redundancy Techniques for Latency Reduction in Cloud Systems. *ACM Trans. Modeling and Perform. Evaluation of Comput. Sys. (TOMPECS)* (to appear, 2017).
[11] Swanand Kadhe, Emina Soljanin, and Alex Sprintson. 2015. Analyzing the download time of availability codes. In *2015 IEEE International Symposium on Information Theory (ISIT).* IEEE, 1467–1471.
[12] Swanand Kadhe, Emina Soljanin, and Alex Sprintson. 2015. When do the availability codes make the stored data more available?. In *2015 53rd Annual Allerton Conference on Communication, Control, and Computing (Allerton).* IEEE, 956–963.
[13] Ankit Singh Rawat, Dimitris S Papailiopoulos, Alexandros G Dimakis, and Sriram Vishwanath. 2014. Locality and availability in distributed storage. In *2014 IEEE International Symposium on Information Theory.* IEEE, 681–685.
[14] Qiqi Shuai and Victor O. K. Li. 2016. Reducing Delay of Flexible Download in Coded Distributed Storage System. In *2016 IEEE Global Communications Conference, GLOBECOM 2016, Washington, DC, USA, December 4-8, 2016.* 1–6.
[15] Itzhak Tamo and Alexander Barg. 2014. A family of optimal locally recoverable codes. *IEEE Transactions on Information Theory* 60, 8 (2014), 4661–4676.

An Empirical Analysis of Facebook's Free Basics Program

Siddharth Singh
IIIT Delhi

Vedant Nanda
IIIT Delhi

Rijurekha Sen
MPI-SWS

Sohaib Ahmad
LUMS

Satadal Sengupta
IIT Kharagpur

Amreesh Phokeer
University of Cape Town

Zaid Ahmed Farooq
LUMS

Taslim Arefin Khan
BUET

Ponnurangam Kumaraguru
IIIT Delhi

Ihsan Ayyub Qazi
LUMS

David Choffnes
North Eastern University

Krishna P. Gummadi
MPI-SWS

ACM Reference format:
Siddharth Singh, Vedant Nanda, Rijurekha Sen, Sohaib Ahmad, Satadal Sengupta, Amreesh Phokeer, Zaid Ahmed Farooq, Taslim Arefin Khan, Ponnurangam Kumaraguru, Ihsan Ayyub Qazi, David Choffnes, and Krishna P. Gummadi. 2017. An Empirical Analysis of Facebook's Free Basics Program. In *Proceedings of ACM Sigmetrics conference, Urbana-Champaign,IL, USA, June 05-09, 2017 (SIGMETRICS '17)*, 2 pages.
https://doi.org/http://dx.doi.org/10.1145/3078505.3078554

1 BACKGROUND

Facebook's Free Basics program offers a set of zero-rated web services, in collaboration with cellular providers in select developing countries [4]. Subscribers of these cellular providers can access Free Basics participating services without incurring data charges by using their mobile phone browsers or via an Android app [2]. The program has grown to more than 60 countries in its first two years [8], with 25 new countries added since May 2016 [10]. These are some of the most densely populated countries in the world [1], with low levels of Internet accessibility but very high rates of mobile phone usage [6, 12]. Facebook claims that Free Basics can bridge this accessibility gap by bringing more people online for free [3] and, therefore, has the potential to bridge the "digital divide" [15].

The program has also created controversy with strong opposition from proponents of an open Internet [7, 13]. They have raised several concerns. First, Facebook alone controls which services are offered in Free Basics, potentially enabling content restrictions in the form of a "walled garden Internet" for its users. Second, Facebook requires that data passes through its proxies in plain text, potentially compromising Free Basics users' privacy. Last, by offering only a subset of Internet services for free, Facebook potentially violates net neutrality by enabling unfair competition between the zero-rated Free Basics services and the paid web services that do not participate in Free Basics. These concerns have caused regulators to take action in some countries [7]; for example, India ultimately banned the service [9, 14]. Even in countries that allow Free Basics, there are questions as to how popular it is [5], and whether it is attracting first-time Internet users as claimed [11].

2 RESEARCH QUESTIONS

In this paper, we develop a suite of measurement techniques to improve the transparency of Free Basics and inform policy debates with empirical evidence. While our study necessarily focuses on Free Basics, our approach can be applied to any similar zero-rated and proxied services that arise. Our analysis answers the following key questions covering different aspects of the program:

- **Free Basics services:** What services constitute the current walled garden of Free Basics? Are these services same across countries? Are these services growing over time?
- **Free Basics users:** How many visitors does a typical service get, and from which countries, demographic and economic backgrounds?
- **Free Basics architecture and Internet providers:** What network quality are the services given, as a trade-off for free access? Which party is primarily responsible for the quality: Facebook or the participating cellular providers?

3 METHODOLOGY

We answer these questions using the following measurement methodology. First, we implement an Android app to scalably collect Free Basics service lists across countries and over time. Second, we deploy our own Free Basics services to understand Facebook's approval and deployment process, and to characterize users who visit our services. Third, we use dedicated clients in Pakistan and South Africa and run controlled experiments against our services, allowing us to characterize the Free Basics proxy architecture, network QoS, caching, and data-encryption policies.

Our main contributions in this paper are as follows:

- We design experiments with multiple vantage points to audit Free Basics.
- We collect empirical data and use them to provide visibility into its services, users, and networks at scale. Our approach can be applied to audit similar programs—be it a global program or one that is ISP-specific (e.g., T-Mobile's Binge On or Videotron's "Unlimited Music").
- We use our observations to evaluate concerns and acclamations about the program to facilitate informed debate.

4 KEY RESULTS

Our measurements provide insight into Free Basics' architecture, users, content providers, and cellular service providers. Specifically, we highlight the following key findings:

- There are currently 200-450 Free Basics services across three countries of Bangladesh, Pakistan and South Africa. Most of the services are country-specific, and they have grown by 100-150 new services over the last nine months.
- One of our Free Basics services Bugle News, an RSS news feed aggregator offered in English, Spanish and French, attracted 49.2K unique visitors from 45+ countries between Sep 2016 and Jan 2017. These users were characterized by both high- and low-end mobile devices, indicating Free Basics being used by its target user population with limited technical means, but also by others who are more well off.
- Free Basics services get 4x–12x worse network throughput than their paid counterparts. We isolate the root causes to network path inflation and bandwidth limits from both Facebook proxies and/or cellular providers.

5 DISCUSSION

One of the main points of opposition of the Free Basics program has been "why do services need Facebook's approval to get enlisted in the Free Basics program?". In our experience of deploying Free Basics services, Facebook's feedback has been strictly technical. Our overall experience has been very positive.

A second point of concern has been "all data will flow through Facebook's proxies". Our deployment experience validates Facebook's advertised architecture of a proxy network. We identify that there are at least two proxy servers on the Free-Basics path between the mobile client and the web server.

A third point of concern has been "some free services included in the program have unfair advantage over other services not part of the program, violating net neutrality". Our measurements show that the download speeds for Free Basics services can be 4-12x worse than their paid counterparts. Further, the performance depends strongly on factors like path inflation between the mobile client and the web server, throttling policies at Facebook proxy servers, and traffic differentiation policies of individual cellular providers. This implies that the net neutrality debate should have more nuance than the "free vs. paid" arguments, asking additional questions like "free, but at what cost?"

A fourth concern has been that it claims "to bring millions of poor and first time Internet users online" [3], while opponents claim "people use it only as a stop gap measure when they run out of data charges" [11]. We analyze the device capabilities from where we receive server requests. Our observations show a mix of relatively expensive high-capability mobile phones, as well as a large number of requests from WAP browsers typically found on low-cost devices. This gives support both in favor of and against the debate.

Finally, in the presence of all concerns about Free Basics, one might ask whether it is contributing to a social good.. Analyzing the currently deployed Free Basics services, we find some excellent services on health, education, social awareness, news and other topics. Moreover, we found that even a simple RSS feed aggregator service on Free Basics can get 49.2K unique visitors within 4 months from 45+ developing countries, as we experienced with Bugle News. Thus creative thinking on how to harness this platform with services might help advance many research objectives targeting a Free Basics user population.

REFERENCES

[1] Dadax. 2017. Worldometers - real time world statistics. http://www.worldometers.info/. (2017).

[2] Facebook. 2015. Free Basics by Facebook - Android Apps on Google Play. https://play.google.com/store/apps/details?id=org.internet&hl=en. (2015).

[3] Facebook. 2016. Brought more than 25 million people online who wouldn't be otherwise. https://info.internet.org/en/blog/2016/05/10/announcing-the-launch-of-free-basics-in-nigeria/. (2016).

[4] Facebook. 2017. internet.org by facebook. https://info.internet.org/en/. (2017).

[5] A4AI Alliance for Affordable Internet. 2016. The Impacts Of Emerging Mobile Data Services In Developing Countries. http://a4ai.org/wp-content/uploads/2016/05/MeasuringImpactsofMobileDataServices_ResearchBrief2.pdf. (2016).

[6] World Bank Group. 2016. World DataBank. http://databank.worldbank.org/data/. (2016).

[7] Anita Gurumurthy and Nandini Chami. 2016. Internet governance as 'ideology in practice' - India's 'Free Basics' controversy. *Journal on Internet Regulation* (2016).

[8] Facebook internet.org. 2017. Where we've launched. https://info.internet.org/en/story/where-weve-launched/. (2017).

[9] Telecom Regulatory Authority of India. 2016. Prohibition of Discriminatory Tariff for Data Services Regulations, 2016. http://www.trai.gov.in/sites/default/files/Regulation_Data_Service.pdf. (2016).

[10] Rijurekha Sen, Hasnain Ali Pirzada, Amreesh Phokeer, Zaid Ahmed Farooq, Satadal Sengupta, David Choffnes, and Krishna P. Gummadi. 2016. On the Free Bridge Across the Digital Divide: Assessing the Quality of Facebook's Free Basics Service. In *Proceedings of the 16th ACM Internet Measurement Conference (IMC)*.

[11] Maeve Shearlaw. 2016. Facebook lures Africa with free internet - but what is the hidden cost? https://www.theguardian.com/world/2016/aug/01/facebook-free-basics-internet-africa-mark-zuckerberg. (2016).

[12] Internet Live Stats. 2016. Internet Users by Country. http://www.internetlivestats.com/internet-users-by-country/. (2016).

[13] OpenMedia Steve Anderson. 2016. Opening Internet.org and Free Basics: An open letter to Facebook. https://openmedia.org/sites/default/files/openmedia-facebook-freebasicsletter.pdf. (2016).

[14] James Vincent. 2016. Facebook's Free Basics service has been banned in India. http://www.theverge.com/2016/2/8/10913398/free-basics-india-regulator-ruling. (2016).

[15] Wikipedia. 2017. Digital divide. https://en.wikipedia.org/wiki/Digital_divide. (2017).

Multipath TCP on a VANET: A Performance Study

Jorge Mena
University of California, Los Angeles
Los, Angeles, CA 90095
jmena@cs.ucla.edu

Peter Bankole
University of California, Los Angeles
Los, Angeles, CA 90095
ptb4866@ucla.edu

Mario Gerla
University of California, Los Angeles
Los, Angeles, CA 90095
gerla@cs.ucla.edu

ABSTRACT

Highly dynamic vehicular networks use long-range radio technologies such as DSRC, WiMAX, and Cellular networks to maintain connectivity. Multipath TCP offers the possibility to combine these radio technologies to improve network performance, allow robust handoffs, and maintain vehicle connectivity at all times. The proliferation of mobile devices with dual interfaces and the manufacturers' interest to make their vehicles smarter and more competitive create the ideal scenario for MPTCP on VANETs. In this paper, we study the performance of MPTCP on two VANET scenarios: Vehicle-to-Infrastructure (V2I), and Vehicle-to-Vehicle, (V2V) under distinct velocities.

CCS CONCEPTS

•Networks →Network performance analysis; Mobile networks; *Network monitoring; Wireless local area networks; Mobile ad hoc networks; Public Internet;*

KEYWORDS

Multipath TCP; MPTCP; VANET; Measurement; Cellular; 4G; LTE; WiFi; Wireless

1 INTRODUCTION

A recently released Cisco VNI forecast [5] predicts that by 2020 traffic from wireless and mobile devices will account for two-thirds of the total IP traffic; smartphones alone will account for 30% of the traffic. Video traffic will take the lion's share with 82%, with content-delivery networks carrying nearly three-fourths of all the traffic. Current smartphone devices are equipped with at least two wireless interfaces: WiFi and LTE. Cellular improvements on LTE rival the performance benefits of WiFi networks; however, LTE coverage may become congested and limited, or carriers may impose data cap limits. Relying solely on LTE connectivity could therefore become prohibitively expensive. In this heterogeneous environment, it is desirable to maximize the use of WiFi coverage whenever available before a connection moves over to Cellular; that is, maximize the cellular traffic offload. Multipath TCP [2] is a backward-compatible evolution of TCP that allows precisely that. MPTCP performs seemless network handovers while devices

SIGMETRICS'17, June 5–9, 2017, Urbana-Champaign, IL, USA
© 2017 Copyright held by the owner/author(s). 978-1-4503-5032-7/17/06.
DOI: http://dx.doi.org/10.1145/3078505.3078555

maintain their connection sessions undisturbed in a *make-before-break* manner. Current implementations today exists in the Apple iOS® [1] and the Linux kernel [4].

2 VEHICULAR AD HOC NETWORKS, VANET

A Vehicular Ad-hoc Network, or VANET [3], is a network of connected vehicles that aim to improve the vehicular traffic safety on the road; other applications include entertainment and content delivery. To coordinate, reliable communication among the vehicles is fundamental; robustness, seamless handover, and backward compatibility are some of the characteristics that makes of MPTCP an ideal candidate. There are two VANET configurations considered in this paper:

Vehicle-to-Infrastructure Communication (V2I). Vehicles may be able to communicate with other vehicles or remote servers via a road-side infrastructure, e. g., access points at street lights or intersections; see Figure 1.

Vehicle-to-Vehicle Communication (V2V). Direct communication between two vehicles over a WLAN, LTE, DSRC, etc., regardless of any roadside infrastructure. They may share their WAN interface, e.g., Cellular or WiMAX; see Figure 2.

3 MULTIPATH TCP, MPTCP

Multipath TCP, or MPTCP [2], is a backward compatible evolution of TCP that provides transport services by transparently leveraging available network connections (WiFi, Cellular, etc.) into a single, coherent service (pooling principle) to upper layer applications. MPTCP goals [6] are throughput improvement, connection robustness and fairness; in general, as a minimum requirement, MPTCP must perform as well as regular TCP in any scenario.

Resource pooling [7] is the main concept behind MPTCP. To achieve the MPTCP goals, the following congestion control algorithms are available: LIA and OLIA; regular TCP can be used but it does not provide fairness. To coordinate the resource coupling, a greedy (*default*) scheduler tries to push as many packets as possible on any path at any time; another scheduler is *round robin*. Path management is simple: if one interface gets connected, MPTCP tries to establish a path through it, this is the *fullmesh*; *ndiffports* and *binder* are other path managers.

4 VEHICULAR TEST BED

Figure 1 and 2 describe two configurations of our testbed. Vehicles are equipped with a laptop that runs Linux and MPTCP v0.90. For V2I configurations, the vehicle connects to the Internet via LTE by a USB tethered smartphone to avoid WiFi interference; it also has a WiFi interface using an external 9dBi antenna. Under V2I, the vehicle connects to either a Roadside Unit, regular WiFi router

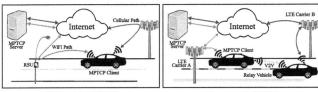

Figure 1: V2I   **Figure 2: V2V**

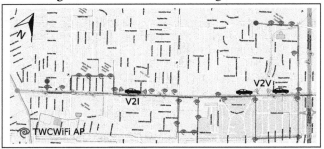

Figure 3: TWCWiFi Map: V2I configuration

static on the roadside, or the Time Warner Cable metropolitan WiFi network in Los Angeles, California. For the V2V configuration, vehicles use an external WiFi antenna that operates under 5.8GHz band, to emulate DSRC, a VANET network technology. Vehicles engaging under V2V communication share their LTE connection to create multiple paths.

5 EXPERIMENT SCENARIOS

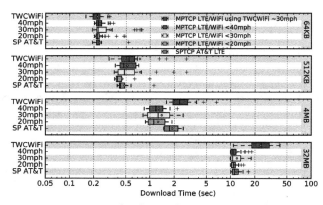

Figure 4: Download time for MPTCP under V2I

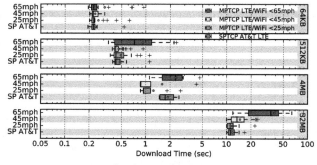

Figure 5: Download time for MPTCP under V2V

Figure 3 shows some of the routes followed on our performance study. The V2I experiments leverage the TWCWiFi metropolitan network of Time Warner Cable and the vehicle couples it with AT&T LTE on the Venice Bl. route in Los Angeles, California. For the V2V experiments, two vehicles connect using a local WLAN and both share their cellular connections.

6 PRELIMINARY RESULTS

Figures 4 and 5 show the MPTCP download time results for V2I and V2V scenarios under distinct velocities and file transfers, compared to Single Path TCP (SP AT&T) over LTE. Our preliminary results show that MPTCP under V2I configuration has similar performance compared to TCP, while constantly handing over WiFi and LTE networks. Under V2V, MPTCP also performed similarly to TCP; however, higher velocities, 65mph, have a detrimental impact on the transfers. This results demonstrates that MPTCP performance does not suffer significant impact under moderate velocities, 45mph in our experiments; at higher speeds, MPTCP performance starts to suffer.

7 CONCLUSION

This paper describes a testbed that studies the performance of MPTCP under two VANET configurations: V2I and V2V. Our current results show that MPTCP performs comparable to SP TCP; this is a significant result since MPTCP allows robust connections with seamless handovers while it maintains comparable performance to TCP. TCP, on the other hand, must either drain the LTE connection, which may be expensive, or disconnect and reconnect during handovers, which degrades performance. However, we found that MPTCP does not currently operate well under very high vehicle velocities in V2V configuration.

ACKNOWLEDGMENTS

This work was supported by The University of California Institute for Mexico and the United States (UC MEXUS) Grant DI-13-140. We would like to acknowledge Katherine Wang and Enrique Segura for their invaluable contributions and help.

REFERENCES

[1] Inc. Apple. 2016. Use Multipath TCP to create backup connections for iOS. https://support.apple.com/en-us/HT201373. (2016).

[2] A. Ford, C. Raiciu, M. Handley, S. Barre, and J. Iyengar. 2011. Architectural Guidelines for Multipath TCP Development. RFC 6182. (March 2011). http://www.ietf.org/rfc/rfc6182.txt

[3] Hannes Hartenstein and Kenneth P. Laberteaux. 2010. *VANET: Vehicular Applications and Inter-Networking Technologies* (1 ed.). Wiley, Chichester, West Sussex, UK.

[4] Multipath-TCP. 2015. Linux Kernel Implementation; v0.90. (June 2015). http://www.multipath-tcp.org

[5] Paper, Cisco White. 2016. Cisco Visual Networking Index: Forecast and Methodology, 2015-2020. (February 2016). http://www.cisco.com/c/en/us/solutions/collateral/service-provider/visual-networking-index-vni/mobile-white-paper-c11-520862.html

[6] C. Raiciu, Paasch C., Barre S., Ford A., Honda M., Duchene F., Bonaventure O., and M. Handley. 2012. How Hard Can It Be? Designing and Implementing a Deployable Multipath TCP. In *Presented as part of the 9th USENIX Symposium on Networked Systems Design and Implementation (NSDI 12)*. USENIX, San Jose, CA, 399–412. https://www.usenix.org/conference/nsdi12/technical-sessions/presentation/raiciu

[7] Damon Wischik, Mark Handley, and Marcelo Bagnulo Braun. 2008. The Resource Pooling Principle. *SIGCOMM Comput. Commun. Rev.* 38, 5 (September 2008), 47–52. DOI:http://dx.doi.org/10.1145/1452335.1452342

A Fast, Small, and Dynamic Forwarding Information Base

Ye Yu
University of Kentucky
ye.yu@uky.edu

Djamal Belazzougui
CERIST
dbelazzougui@cerist.dz

Chen Qian
UC Santa Cruz
cqian12@ucsc.edu

Qin Zhang
Indiana University
qzhangcs@indiana.edu

ABSTRACT

Concise is a Forwarding information base (FIB) design that uses very little memory to support fast query of a large number of dynamic network names or flow IDs. Concise makes use of minimal perfect hashing and the SDN framework to design and implement the data structure, protocols, and system. Experimental results show that Concise uses significantly smaller memory to achieve faster query speed compared to existing FIB solutions and it can be updated very efficiently.

ACM Reference format:
Ye Yu, Djamal Belazzougui, Chen Qian, and Qin Zhang. 2017. A Fast, Small, and Dynamic Forwarding Information Base. In *Proceedings of SIGMETRICS '17, June 5-9, 2017, Urbana-Champaign, IL, USA,* , 2 pages.
DOI: http://dx.doi.org/10.1145/3078505.3078556

1 INTRODUCTION

A Forwarding Information Base (FIB) is a data structure, typically a table, that is used to determine the proper forwarding actions for packets, at the data plane of a forwarding device (e.g, switch or router). There are two main reasons to cause the *FIB explosion* problem: *1)* the increased population of modern networks such as the Internet, data center networks, and Internet of Things (IoT); *2)* the use of layer-two semantics and location-independent host names (or device IDs, flow IDs, flow tags, etc.) in new network architectures, such as SDN [6], SDX [1], IoT, Metro Ethernet [3], LTE, and MobilityFirst [4]. Location-independent names are difficult to aggregate.

We present a generalized and portable solution to solve the FIB size problem at any forwarding devices. The proposed FIB structure, called Concise, achieves *fast queries* with *memory-efficiency* and provides the support of various newly proposed network architectures and protocols on memory-limited forwarding devices. It significantly improves the capability of using general-purpose platforms for network processing, such as virtual switches and virtual network functions.

Concise has the following properties.

(1) Compared to existing FIB designs for name switching, Concise supports *much faster name lookup* using *significantly smaller memory*, shown by both theoretical analysis and empirical studies.
(2) Concise can be efficiently updated to reflect network dynamics. Results show that a single CPU core is able to perform millions of network-wide updates per second. Concise makes the control plane highly scalable.
(3) Concise guarantees to return the correct forwarding actions for valid names. It is *not* probabilistic like those using Bloom filters [5].
(4) Unlike recently proposed forwarding engines[6], which are specifically designed for customized and high-end hardware platforms, Concise is a *portable solution*, and it can be used on either software or hardware switches.

2 DESIGN OF CONCISE

A new classification structure Othello. Concise is built on a data structure Othello designed by us. Othello was motivated by minimal perfect hashing (MPH) [2]. The Othello data structure and Concise supports fast query and update (addition/deletion of names). In the resource-limited switches (data plane), Concise only includes the query component and is optimized for memory efficiency and query speed. The construction and update components are moved to the resource-rich control plane. Concise is constructed and updated in the control plane and transmitted to the data plane. It is the first work to implement minimum perfect hashing schemes to network applications with update functionalities. We do not consider address aggregation.

For a packet with ID/name k, the FIB returns an integer i representing a forwarding action A_i. A_i may be "forward to a specified port" or "drop". We assume the controller knows the set S of all names in the network. In addition, Concise only accepts queries of valid names, i.e., $k \in S$. We assume that firewalls or similar network functions are installed at ingress switches to filter packets whose IDs do not exist.

Let S be the set of all names. $n = |S|$. An Othello classifies n names into two disjoint sets X and Y: $X \cup Y = S$ and $X \cap Y = \varnothing$. An Othello is a seven-tuple $\langle m_a, m_b, h_a, h_b, \boldsymbol{a}, \boldsymbol{b}, G \rangle$.

- Integers m_a and m_b. m_a is the smallest power of 2 such that $m_a \geq 1.33n$ and $m_b = m_a$.
- Uniform random hash $\langle h_a, h_b \rangle$, mapping k to integers $\{0, 1, \cdots, m_a - 1\}$ and $\{0, 1, \cdots, m_b - 1\}$, respectively.
- Bitmaps $\boldsymbol{a}$ and $\boldsymbol{b}$ in lengths m_a and m_b respectively.
- A bipartite graph G. During Othello construction and update, G is used to determine the values in $\boldsymbol{a}$ and $\boldsymbol{b}$.

The Othello query structure only includes $\langle h_a, h_b \rangle$, $\boldsymbol{a}$, and $\boldsymbol{b}$, taking less than $4n + O(1)$ bits memory. For a name k, it computes $\tau(k) = \boldsymbol{a}[h_a(k)] \oplus \boldsymbol{b}[h_b(k)]$. If $\tau(k) = 0$, $k \in X$. If $\tau(k) = 1$, $k \in Y$. If $k \notin S$, $\tau(k)$ returns 0 or 1 arbitrarily.

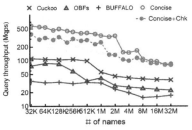

Figure 1: FIB throughput

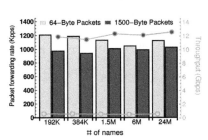

Figure 2: Performance on DPDK

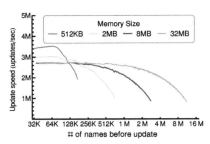

Figure 3: Update speed of Concise

In Othello control structure, $G = (U, V, E)$ is an acyclic bipartite graph, used to decide the values in a and b, so that the query $\tau(k)$ returns the correct result. Each edge in E represents a name. There is a edge $(u_i, v_j) \in E$ if and only if there is a name $k \in S$ such that $h_a(k) = i$ and $h_b(k) = j$. Note that G is a representation of MPH *if G is acyclic*. We prove that the *expected* time to construct an Othello control structure with n names is $O(n)$ and the expected time to add/delete/alter a name is $O(1)$.

Extending Othello for FIB. The extension of Othello to support classification for more than two sets is called a Parallel Othello Group (POG). An l-POG is able to classify names into 2^l disjoint sets. It serves as a FIB with 2^l forwarding actions. Note all l Othellos share the same S and $\langle h_a, h_b \rangle$. Since the edges in G is determined by only $S = X \cup Y$ and $\langle h_a, h_b \rangle$, they also share a same G. Hence we propose to use two vectors A and B, containing m_a and m_b l-bit integers respectively. Let $A[i]$ be the i-th element of A. The t-th least significant bit of $A[i]$ is $a_t[i]$, where a_t is a bitmap of the t-th Othello query structure. B is defined similarly. Hence, $\tau(k)$ can be computed by: $\tau(k) = A[h_a(k)] \oplus B[h_b(k)]$. When l is not larger than the word size of the platform, each l-POG query only requires two memory accesses for fetching $A[i]$ and $B[j]$. On 64-bit platforms, a 64-POG is sufficient to support name switching with 2^{64} sets of actions. As a result a Concise *only requires two memory accesses* for each lookup.

We also design the update protocol of Concise.

3 EVALUATION

We implement Concise on three different platforms and conduct extensive experiments to evaluate its performance, including 1) a memory-mode of the POG query and control structures, running on different cores of a desktop computer; 2) a Concise prototype on Click; and 3) a Concise prototype on DPDK. We compare Concise with two most recent scalable FIBs: Cuckoo hashing [6] and BUFFALO [5].

Table 1 shows the size of memory of POG, Cuckoo hash table, and BUFFALO, for various types of names: MAC, IPv4, IPv6, and OpenFlow. The memory space used by Concise is significantly smaller than that of Cuckoo and BUFFALO. It is only determined by the number of names n and the number of actions, and is independent of the name lengths.

Fig. 1 shows the query throughput. The names are MAC addresses (48-bit). When n is smaller than 2 million, the

FIB Example			Memory Size		
Name Type	# Names	# Act.	Concise	Cukoo	BUFFALO
MAC (48 bits)	7×10^5	16	1M	5.62M	2.64M
MAC (48 bits)	5×10^6	256	16M	40.15M	27.70M
MAC (48 bits)	3×10^7	256	96M	321.23M	166.23M
IPv4 (32 bits)	1×10^6	16	1.5M	4.27M	3.77M
IPv6 (128 bits)	2×10^6	256	4M	34.13M	11.08M
OpenFlow (356b)	3×10^5	256	1M	14.46M	1.67M
OpenFlow (356b)	1.4×10^6	65536	8M	67.46M	18.21M

Table 1: Memory cost comparison

throughput of Concise is very high (> 400M queries per second (Mqps)). It is because the memory required by Concise is smaller than the cache size (8M for our machine). When $n \geq$ 2M, the throughput decreases but still around 100 Mqps. On the other hand, Cuckoo has the highest throughput among the remaining three FIBs but its throughput is only about only 20% to 50% of that of Concise.

We measure the throughput of the Concise prototype on DPDK. The barchart in Fig. 2 shows that Concise is able to generate, forward, and receive more than 1M packets per second, for both 64-Byte and 1500-Byte packets.

Figure 3 shows the update speed of Concise. We set four memory limits and vary the number of names before update. It is clear that when the n to memory size ratio becomes bigger, the update speed decreases. In all cases, the update speed is very fast (> 1M updates per second), which is sufficient for very large networks.

ACKNOWLEDGEMENT

We thank the suggestions from Kenneth Calvert. Chen Qian was supported by NSF CNS-1701681. Qin Zhang was supported in part by NSF CCF-1525024 and IIS-1633215.

REFERENCES

[1] A. Gupta and others. 2014. SDX: a software defined internet exchange. In *Proc. ACM SIGCOMM*.
[2] B. S. Majewski, NC Wormald, G Havas, and ZJ Czech. 1996. A Family of Perfect Hashing Methods. *Comput. J.* (jun 1996).
[3] Chen Qian and Simon Lam. 2012. ROME: Routing On Metropolitan-scale Ethernet. In *Proc. of IEEE ICNP*.
[4] D. Raychaudhuri, K. Nagaraja, and A. Venkataramani. 2012. MobilityFirst: A Robust and Trustworthy Mobility Centric Architecture for the Future Internet. *MC2R* (2012).
[5] M Yu, A Fabrikant, and J Rexford. 2009. BUFFALO: Bloom filter forwarding architecture for large organizations. In *Proc. of ACM CoNEXT*.
[6] D Zhou, B Fan, H Lim, M Kaminsky, and D G Anderson. 2013. Scalable, High Performance Ethernet Forwarding with Cuckoo-Switch. In *Proc. of ACM CoNEXT*.

HFTraC: High-Frequency Traffic Control

Ning Wu
Cornell University
nw276@cornell.edu

Yingjie Bi
Cornell University
yb236@cornell.edu

Nithin Michael
Waltz Networks, Inc.
nithin@waltznetworks.com

Ao Tang
Cornell University
atang@ece.cornell.edu

John Doyle
California Institute of Technology
doyle@caltech.edu

Nikolai Matni
California Institute of Technology
nmatni@caltech.edu

ABSTRACT

We propose high-frequency traffic control (HFTraC), a rate control scheme that coordinates the transmission rates and buffer utilizations in routers network-wide at fast timescale. HFTraC can effectively deal with traffic demand fluctuation by utilizing available buffer space in routers network-wide, and therefore lead to significant performance improvement in terms of tradeoff between bandwidth utilization and queueing delay. We further note that the performance limit of HFTraC is determined by the network architecture used to implement it. We provide trace-driven evaluation of the performance of HFTraC implemented in the proposed architectures that vary from fully centralized to completely decentralized.

KEYWORDS

Network control and management; Communication networks

ACM Reference format:
Ning Wu, Yingjie Bi, Nithin Michael, Ao Tang, John Doyle, and Nikolai Matni. 2017. HFTraC: High-Frequency Traffic Control. In *Proceedings of SIGMETRICS '17, Urbana-Champaign, IL, USA, June 05-09, 2017,* 3 pages.
DOI: http://dx.doi.org/10.1145/3078505.3078557

1 INTRODUCTION

Due to the network dynamics induced by both varying traffic demand and resource supply, responsive approaches of network control that update network configurations at a fast timescale becomes increasingly appealing. The goal of such approaches is to improve resource utilization by reacting to network changes, rather than by over provisioning with respect to its typical behavior. The emergence of Software-Defined Networking (SDN) [5] not only makes it more feasible for network control and management technology to operate at higher frequency, but also enables the flexibility of their architecture design.

In this work, we propose high-frequency traffic control (HF-TraC) that dynamically controls, at around RTT timescales, the link service rate from in-network routers based on the information exchange with each other including queue length and transmission rate. HFTraC targets at better utilizing available buffer space

SIGMETRICS '17, June 05-09, 2017, Urbana-Champaign, IL, USA
© 2017 Copyright held by the owner/author(s).
ACM ISBN 978-1-4503-5032-7/17/06.
DOI: http://dx.doi.org/10.1145/3078505.3078557

and thus achieving higher network utilization and smaller average buffer size than static rate-limiting policies. The feature that HF-TraC works by only rate-limiting the routers' interface and does not change queuing management or routing strategy allows its compatibility with any standard AQM schemes [3, 7] and TE approaches [2, 4]. The scheme of information exchanging among the routers has an important effect on the responsiveness which determines the system performance at the time-scale that we consider. Therefore we further provide four different implementation architectures of HFTraC, varying from completely centralized to completely decentralized, and evaluate the associated latency/performance tradeoff.

2 DESIGN

We consider a network consisting of a set of switches V and a set of directed links L. We let $\mathcal{L}_v^{in}$ and $\mathcal{L}_v^{out}$ denote the set of incoming and outgoing links respectively for a switch $v \in V$. The network is shared by a set I of source-destination (SD) pairs and the traffic demand is denoted as d_i for SD pair $i \in I$. Let x_l^i be the arrival rate into the egress buffer associated with link l and let f_l^i be the transmission rate on link l due to SD pair i. Switch v splits flows along outgoing links according to split ratios $\alpha_{l,v}^i$ satisfying $\sum_{l \in \mathcal{L}_v^{out}} \alpha_{l,v}^i = 1$ for each SD pair i that utilizes link l. To capture the effect of traffic fluctuations, we model the demand fluctuation $\Delta d_i(t)$ at time t as $\Delta d_i(t) = d_i(t) - d_i^*$, where d_i^* is the average demand over a TE update interval. Similarly, the fluctuation of arrival and transmission rates are given by $\Delta x_l^i(t) = x_l^i(t) - (x_l^i)^*$ and $\Delta f_l^i(t) = f_l^i(t) - (f_l^i)^*$. The fluctuation of aggregated arrival rate and transmission rate on link l are defined as $\Delta x_l(t) = \sum_{i \in I} \Delta x_l^i(t)$ and $\Delta f_l(t) = \sum_{i \in I} \Delta f_l^i(t)$ respectively.

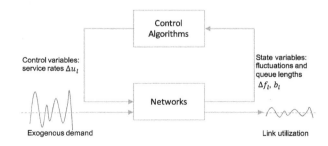

Figure 1: HFTraC Feedback Control System

We construct the feedback control system of HFTraC shown in Fig 1. The control variables in the system are the changes of service rate $\Delta u_l(t)$, and the control action is done by rate limiting link l to the dynamic service rate $u_l(t) = (f_l)^* + \Delta u_l(t)$. The state variables are the network state information including transmission rate fluctuations $\Delta f_l(t)$ and queue lengths $b_l(t)$. The control algorithm outputs the service rate change $\Delta u_l(t)$ for each link at RTT timescales, taking the measurement of state variables as input. The service rates under the dynamic control will in turn affect the current network state.

We pose the discrete-time optimal control problem as:

$$\min_{\Delta u_l(n)} \quad \lim_{n\to\infty} \sum_l [\mathbb{E}[\Delta f_l(n)]^2 + \lambda_l \mathbb{E}[b_l(n)]^2]$$
$$\text{s.t.} \quad b_l(n+1) = b_l(n) + \tau(\Delta x_l(n) - \Delta u_l(n)),$$
$$\Delta f_l(n+1) = \Delta u_l(n),$$
$$\Delta x_l(n) = \sum_{i\in I} \Delta x_l^i(n),$$
$$\Delta x_l^i(n) = \begin{cases} \Delta d_i(n) & \text{if } l \text{ is edge link,} \\ \alpha_{l,v}^i \sum_{k\in \mathcal{L}_v^{\text{in}}} \beta_k^i \Delta f_k(n - n_k) & \text{otherwise,} \end{cases}$$
$$\Delta u_l(n) = \gamma_l(I_l(n)) \text{ for all } l \in L.$$

The objective function is a weighted sum (specified by the weights $\lambda_l \geq 0$) of the variance in transmission rate and buffer length. τ is the sampling interval satisfying $\tau n_k = \delta_k$ for some integers n_k. We make the simplifying assumption that $\Delta f_l^i(n) = \Delta f_l(n)\beta_l^i$ where $\beta_l^i := \frac{(f_l^i)^*}{\sum_{k\in I}(f_l^k)^*}$. The service rate is constrained by $I_l(n)$, which is the set of state information available to the algorithm taking the control loop latency into account, i.e.

$$I_l(n) := \{(b_k(n - n_{lk}))_{k\in L}, (\Delta f_k(n - n_{lk}))_{k\in L}\},$$

where n_{lk} is taken to be the communication delay imposed on information exchange from link k to link l. The communication delays vary in different architecture, thus driving us to the exploration of architecture design. Here we define four candidate architectures that range from completely centralized to fully decentralized.

The GOD architecture: The Globally Optimal Delay free (GOD) architecture assumes that a logically and physically centralized controller can instantaneously access global network states as well as compute and execute control laws Δu_l for each router. It is clearly not implementable in practice, but it represents a benchmark against which all other architectures should be compared.

The centralized architecture: A logically and physically centralized controller makes control decisions. The control loop latency is determined by $n_{\max} = \max_{l\in L} n_{lk}$, the longest RTT from any router to the centralized controller. It takes $\frac{1}{2}n_{\max}$ for the controller to collect complete network information and another $\frac{1}{2}n_{\max}$ for the router to receive the control decisions.

The coordinated architecture: The controller is logically and physically distributed, with each local controller computing Δu_l based on shared network state information. n_{lk} are specified by the delays of collecting network state information at router associated with link l. The local control actions will be taken immediately once being computed by the controller with the knowledge of timely local information and delayed shared information.

The myopic architecture: This is a completely decentralized architecture, in which local controllers compute their control laws Δu_l using local information only, i.e., the delays available to the controller associated with link l satisfy $n_{ll} = 0, n_{lk} = \infty$.

3 RESULTS

We here provide our trace-driven evaluation results of HFTraC on a triangle topology with three nodes running Open vSwitch (OVS) [6]. Links between the switches have capacity of 30 Mbps, RTT of 20 ms and buffer limit of 0.2 Mbits. There is one host node connecting to each of the switch. Edge links that connects the switch and host have larger capacity of 42 Mbps and buffer limit of 0.3 Mbits. The real Internet traces are extracted from CAIDA anonymized dataset [1] recorded with nanosecond scale timestamps. We replay the trace data on the topology from a source host to a destination host. Given by the routing solution to some TE method, 75% of the traffic is transmitted on the shorter path with a single hop, and 25% is transmitted on the longer path with two hops. We choose a sampling time of $\tau = 10$ ms – hence, the control laws are updated once every 10 ms.

We evaluate how the total loss rate and average queue length change as maximum link utilization is increased in GOD, centralized, myopic and coordinated schemes and compare the performance with the standard FIFO scheme which is in fact static rate limiting by link capacity. Fig. 2 shows that HFTraCs are able to reduce packet loss by absorbing some of the traffic demand randomness into the buffers – not surprisingly, this in general leads to slightly larger queue length when HFTraC is used. Thus we see that HFTraC, regardless of architecture, effectively reduces the packet loss rate especially when link utilization is over 85%.

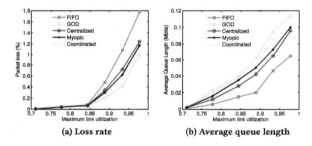

(a) Loss rate　　　(b) Average queue length

Figure 2: Trace-driven evaluation of HFTraC.

REFERENCES

[1] *The CAIDA UCSD Anonymized Internet Traces - February 2012.* http://www.caida.org/data/passive/passive_2012_dataset.xml.
[2] Anwar Elwalid, Cheng Jin, Steven Low, and Indra Widjaja. MATE: MPLS adaptive traffic engineering. In *Proceedings of IEEE INFOCOM*, pages 1300–1309, 2001.
[3] Sally Floyd and Van Jacobson. Random early detection gateways for congestion avoidance. *IEEE/ACM Transactions on Networking (ToN)* 1(4):397–413, 1993.
[4] Sushant Jain, Alok Kumar, Subhasree Mandal, Joon Ong, Leon Poutievski, Arjun Singh, Subbaiah Venkata, Jim Wanderer, Junlan Zhou, Min Zhu, and others. B4: Experience with a globally-deployed software defined WAN. *ACM SIGCOMM Computer Communication Review* 43(4):3–14, 2013.
[5] Bob Lantz, Brandon Heller, and Nick McKeown. A network in a laptop: rapid prototyping for software-defined networks. In *Proceedings of the 9th ACM SIGCOMM Workshop on Hot Topics in Networks*, 2010.
[6] Ben Pfaff, Justin Pettit, Teemu Koponen, Ethan J Jackson, Andy Zhou, Jarno Rajahalme, Jesse Gross, Alex Wang, Joe Stringer, Pravin Shelar, and others. The Design and Implementation of Open vSwitch. In *Proceedings of NSDI*, pages 117–130, 2015.
[7] Kadangode Ramakrishnan and Sally Floyd. *A proposal to add explicit congestion notification (ECN) to IP.* Technical Report, 1998.

Adaptive TTL-Based Caching for Content Delivery

Soumya Basu
The University of Texas at Austin

Aditya Sundarrajan
University of Massachusetts Amherst

Javad Ghaderi
Columbia University

Sanjay Shakkottai
The University of Texas at Austin

Ramesh Sitaraman
University of Massachusetts Amherst,
Akamai Technologies

ABSTRACT

Content Delivery Networks (CDNs) cache and serve a majority of the user-requested content on the Internet, including web pages, videos, and software downloads. We propose two TTL-based caching algorithms that *automatically* adapt to the heterogeneity, burstiness, and non-stationary nature of real-world content requests. The first algorithm called d-TTL dynamically adapts a TTL parameter using a stochastic approximation approach and achieves a given feasible target hit rate. The second algorithm called f-TTL uses two caches, each with its own TTL. The lower-level cache adaptively filters out non-stationary content, while the higher-level cache stores frequently-accessed stationary content. We implement d-TTL and f-TTL and evaluate both algorithms using an extensive nine-day trace consisting of more than 500 million requests from a production CDN server. We show that both d-TTL and f-TTL converge to their hit rate targets with an error of about 1.3%. We also show that f-TTL requires a significantly smaller cache size than d-TTL to achieve the same hit rate, since it effectively filters out rarely-accessed content.

KEYWORDS

TTL caching, Content Delivery Network, Stochastic Approximation

ACM Reference format:
Soumya Basu, Aditya Sundarrajan, Javad Ghaderi, Sanjay Shakkottai, and Ramesh Sitaraman. 2017. Adaptive TTL-Based Caching for Content Delivery. In *Proceedings of SIGMETRICS '17, June 5–9, 2017, Urbana-Champaign, IL, USA, ,* 2 pages.
DOI: http://dx.doi.org/10.1145/3078505.3078560

1 INTRODUCTION

By caching and delivering content to millions of end users around the world, content delivery networks (CDNs) are an integral part of the Internet infrastructure. The major technical challenge in designing caching algorithms for a modern CDN is *adapting* to heterogeneous, bursty (correlations over time) and non-stationary/transient request statistics. In this effort, applying known heuristics such as Che's approximation fail due to modeling inaccuracies and manually tuning the caching algorithms becomes prohibitively expensive. Thus, our goal is to devise self-tuning TTL-based caching algorithms that can automatically learn and adapt to heterogeneous,

bursty and non-stationary traffic and provably achieve any feasible hit rate and cache size.

We propose two TTL-based algorithms: d-TTL (for "dynamic TTL") and f-TTL (for "filtering TTL"). Rather than statically deriving the required TTL values from the request statistics, our algorithms *incrementally adapt* the TTL values after each request, based on the current request patterns. Our algorithms do not have prior knowledge of request statistics; instead we use a stochastic approximation framework and ideas from actor-critic algorithms for parameter adaptation. We implement both d-TTL and f-TTL algorithms and evaluate them using an extensive nine-day trace consisting of more than 500 million requests from a production Akamai CDN server. For a range of object hit rate targets, both d-TTL and f-TTL converge to that target with an error of about 1.3%. For a range of byte hit rate targets, both d-TTL and f-TTL converge to that target with an error that ranges from 0.3% to 2.3%. In particular, f-TTL requires a cache that is 49%(resp., 39%) smaller than d-TTL to achieve the same object hit rate(resp., byte hit rate).

2 TTL-BASED CACHING ALGORITHMS

A TTL-based caching algorithm works as follows. When a new object is requested, it is placed in cache and associated with a time-to-live (TTL) value. If no new request is received for that object, the TTL value is decremented in real-time and the object is evicted when the TTL becomes zero. If a cached object is requested, a *cache hit* occurs and the TTL is reset to its original value. When the requested object is not found in cache, a *cache miss* occurs. Consider T different types of content. The *objective* of this work is to (asymptotically) achieve a *target hit rate* $h_t^* \in (0, 1)$ and a (feasible) *target size rate* s_t^*, for each type $t \in [T]$. To accurately model CDN traffic, we allow the request traffic to be non-independent and non-stationary; the request traffic can have Markovian dependence over time. The traffic comprises a mix of stationary demands (statistics invariant over the timescale of interest), and non-stationary demands (finitely many requests, or in general requests with an asymptotically vanishing request rate). The complete model is described in [1].

d-TTL Cache. The d-TTL algorithm adapts the TTL value on every request arrival to achieve a target hit rate h_t^* $\forall t \in [T]$. d-TTL uses stochastic approximation to dynamically increase the TTL when the current hit rate is below the target, and decrease the TTL when the current hit rate is above the target. Let $\theta_t(l)$ be the TTL value after the l-th request arrival for content type t. Then, if the object experiences a cache miss, d-TTL increases the TTL to, $\theta_t(l+1) = \theta_t(l) + \frac{\eta_0}{l^\alpha}(h_t^*)$, where η_0 is some constant and $\alpha \in (0.5, 1)$.

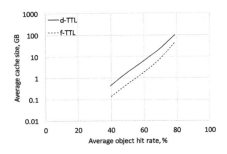

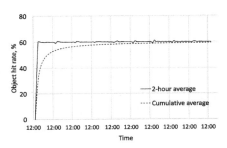

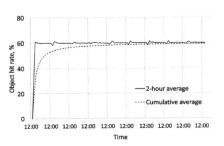

Figure 1: Hit rate curve for object hit rates.

Figure 2: Object hit rate convergence over time for d-TTL; target hit rate=60%.

Figure 3: Object hit rate convergence over time for f-TTL; target hit rate=60%.

On the contrary, in the event of cache hit, the TTL decreases to $\theta_t(l+1) = \theta_t(l) - \frac{\eta_0}{l^\alpha}(1 - h_t^*)$.

While d-TTL does a good job of achieving the target hit rate, it does this at the expense of caching rare and unpopular recurring content for an extended period of time, thus causing an increase in cache size without any significant contribution towards the cache hit rate. We present a two-level adaptive TTL algorithm called filtering TTL (f-TTL) that filters out rare and unpopular content to achieve both a target size rate and a target hit rate (at a cache size smaller than d-TTL).

f-TTL Cache. The two-level f-TTL algorithm maintains two caches, a lower-level cache C_s and a higher-level cache C. To facilitate the filtering process, it uses two dynamic TTL values—one ($\theta_t^s(l)$) less than or equal to the other ($\theta_t(l)$). Upon a *cache miss* for object c of type t, object c, potentially unpopular, is cached in C_s with the smaller TTL to ensure quick eviction. Its metadata $\tilde{c}$ (only the object ID and not the actual content) is cached in C_s with the larger TTL to retain *memory* of this request. The two TTLs are then updated to, $\theta_t^s(l+1) = \theta_t^s(l) + \frac{\eta_0}{l}\left(s_t^* - \theta_t^s(l)\right)$ and $\theta_t(l+1) = \theta_t(l) + \frac{\eta_0}{l^\alpha}h_t^*$.

Upon a *cache hit*, object c—now showing signs of popularity—is cached[1] in the higher-level cache C with the larger TTL, $\theta_t(l)$. Let ϕ be the remaining time for object c. Then, the smaller TTL is updated to $\theta_t^s(l+1) = \theta_t^s(l) + \frac{\eta_0}{l}\left(s_t^* - \theta_t(l) + \phi\right)$ and the larger TTL is decremented to $\theta_t(l+1) = \theta_t(l) - \frac{\eta_0}{l^\alpha}(1 - h_t^*)$.

In f-TTL there is a third possibility. When the requested object c is not in either cache but its metadata $\tilde{c}$ exists, a *virtual hit* occurs. Object c, which is possibly popular is then cached in the higher-level cache with the larger TTL value. The smaller TTL is updated to $\theta_t^s(l+1) = \theta_t^s(l) + \frac{\eta_0}{l}\left(s_t^* - \theta_t(l)\right)$ and the larger TTL increases to $\theta_t(l+1) = \theta_t(l) + \frac{\eta_0}{l^\alpha}h_t^*$.

The extra *memory* in the form of object metadata helps f-TTL cache popular objects for a longer period of time while filtering out rare and unpopular content quickly. Thus, f-TTL utilizes the cache space more efficiently to simultaneously achieve a target hit rate and a target size rate.

The convergence results of both d-TTL and f-TTL algorithms are presented in [1].

3 EMPIRICAL EVALUATION

We use an extensive data set containing access logs for content requested by users that we collected from a typical production server in Akamai's commercially-deployed CDN, over a period of 9 days. The content requests traces contain 504 million requests (resp., 165TB) for 25 million distinct objects (resp., 15TB). We observe that the content popularity distribution exhibits a "long tail" with nearly 70% of the objects accessed only once. Further, we also see that 80% of the requests are for 1% of the objects. This indicates the presence of a significant amount of non-stationary traffic in the form of "one-hit-wonders" and rarely accessed content.

The performance of a caching algorithm is often measured by its hit rate curve (HRC) that relates the cache size to the hit rate it achieves. We compare the HRCs of d-TTL and f-TTL for object hit rates and show that f-TTL significantly outperforms d-TTL by filtering out the rarely-accessed non-stationary content. The HRCs for object hit rates are shown in Figure 1. Note that the y-axis is presented in log scale for clarity.

From Figure 1 we see that f-TTL always performs better than d-TTL. We find that on average, f-TTL requires a cache that is 49% smaller than d-TTL to achieve the same object hit rate.

For the dynamic TTL algorithms to be useful in practice, they need to converge to the target hit rate with low error. From Figures 2 and 3, we see that the 2 hour averaged object hit rates achieved by both d-TTL and f-TTL have a cumulative error of less than 1.3% while achieving the target object hit rate, on average. We also see that both d-TTL and f-TTL converge to the target hit rate quickly, which illustrates that both d-TTL and f-TTL are able to adapt well to the dynamics of the non-stationary traffic.

A more detailed evaluation of the dynamic TTL algorithms including the analysis of byte hit rates, sensitivity analyses and comparison to the Che's approximation heuristic can be found in [1].

ACKNOWLEDGMENTS

This work is partially supported by the US DoT supported D-STOP Tier 1 University Transportation Center, NSF grant CNS-1652115 and NSF grant CNS-1413998.

REFERENCES

[1] Soumya Basu, Aditya Sundarrajan, Javad Ghaderi, Sanjay Shakkottai, and Ramesh Sitaraman. 2017. Adaptive TTL-Based Caching for Content Delivery. *CoRR* abs/1704.04448 (2017). http://arxiv.org/abs/1704.04448

---

[1]Caching an object in the higher-level cache implies evicting the object and/or its metadata from the lower-level cache.

Online Optimization for Markets and the Cloud: Theory and Practice

Abstract of SIGMETRICS 2017 Keynote Talk

Vahab Mirrokni

Google Research, New York

Internet applications provide challenging dynamic environments for applying online optimization techniques. In this talk, I will discuss a number of such problems that we have encountered in the past couple of years at Google in the context of online advertising markets, and in serving cloud services, discuss technical challenges in these areas (with a focus on more recent and ongoing work), and state a number of open problems in these areas.

1 ONLINE OPTIMIZATION IN ADVERTISING APPLICATIONS

For online markets, we mainly discuss problems in the area of online advertising. Online advertising eco-system provides a great platform for a variety of research problems in online stochastic optimization, revenue management, and computational economics (see [KMN15] for a survey of such problems in display ads). Online ads are delivered in a real-time fashion under uncertainty in an environment with strategic agents. Making such real-time (or online) decisions without knowing the future is challenging for repeated auctions.

1.1 Robust Ad Allocation

Given a set of contracts to be fulfilled in an online advertising system, the central optimization problem in ad serving is to select which ad(s) to serve each user while satisfying all the contracts or while maximizing the revenue from these contracts subject to budget or delivery constraints. An important step towards designing an effective algorithm for the assignment of ads to the users is modeling the users' arrivals. One can consider adversarial or stochastic arrival models [FKM+09, FHK+10]. In practice, the input to the allocation problem is rarely adversarial. At the same time, forecasts are not perfect; in fact, sudden spikes in traffic (for example, due to breaking news events) are not uncommon. While ad serving systems have good forecasts for future traffic, they cannot forecast precisely like a stochastic arrival models may suggest. Possibly the most important direction for future research is designing algorithms that can use accurate forecasts to obtain an assignment that beats the worst-case bounds, while maintaining a good performance even when the forecasts turn out to be extremely inaccurate. In this context, we will first highlight the practical importance of considering hybrid models that can take advantage of forecasting, and at the same time, are robust against adversarial changes in the input. I will then discuss our recent results combining stochastic and adversarial input models. In one recent work, we develop simultaneous approximation algorithms for adversarial and stochastic models[MGZ12]: we study online algorithms that achieve a good performance in both adversarial and stochastic arrival models. In another paper, we develop a mixed model for stochastic and adversarial models, and develop algorithms with approximation factors that change as a function of the accuracy of the forecast[EKM15].

1.2 Bank Account Dynamic Auctions for Stateful Pricing

The bulk of online ads are sold via repeated auctions. This is in contrast to a large portion of (display) ads that is sold via traditional contract-based advertising. While several attempts have been made to design new types of contracts that are more suitable for new trends in display advertising[KLN13, MN17], auction-based advertising has several advantages; above all, it allows for more number of advertisers to enter the market with much less long-term commitment. On the other hand, contract-based advertising can offer better welfare and revenue opportunities for sellers and buyers in the market[MN17]. Instead of optimizing these auctions separately per auction, one can design stateful (dynamic) pricing and allocation strategies that may optimize these auctions together. The goal of such dynamic auctions would be to achieve revenue and welfare of contracts while keeping advantages of repeated auctions. While dynamic mechanism design has been an active research area, most of the existing mechanisms are either too computationally complex, or rely too much on forecasting of the future auctions.To address these issues, we discuss results concerning online bundling schemes that can be applied to repeated auction environments. In particular, I will discuss a new family of dynamic mechanisms, called bank account mechanisms [MLTZ16b, MLTZ16a], and show their effectiveness in designing non-clairvoyant dynamic mechanisms that can be implemented without relying on forecasting the future [MLTZ16a], and also dynamic mechanisms with low regret [MLRZ17]. In all these results, we attempt to design simple-to-implement repeated auctions that satisfy ex-post individual rationality and dynamic incentive compatibility. I will further discuss dynamic auctions for Martingale utilities [BML17] that go beyond satisfying ex-post individual rationality and ensure more stable utility for buyers across time.

In addition, I will discuss two sources of stateful-ness in repeated auctions seeking to meet a global constraint while serving ads in a repeated auction environment: one source is in satisfying global budget constraints across all auctions [BBW13, BKMM17]. The other source of statefulness arises in satisfying certain revenue

Permission to make digital or hard copies of part or all of this work for personal or classroom use is granted without fee provided that copies are not made or distributed for profit or commercial advantage and that copies bear this notice and the full citation on the first page. Copyrights for third-party components of this work must be honored. For all other uses, contact the owner/author(s).

SIGMETRICS '17, June 5–9, 2017, Urbana-Champaign, IL, USA

© 2017 Copyright held by the owner/author(s). ACM ISBN 978-1-4503-5032-7/17/06.

DOI: http://dx.doi.org/10.1145/3078505.3078507

sharing properties between publishers selling their page-views and an ad exchange that play an intermediary role in the market [GM14, BLM$^+$17].

2 ONLINE OPTIMIZATION IN SERVING CLOUD SERVICES

For problems on the cloud, I will touch upon a couple of online load balancing problems. The first problem is in the context of consistent hashing with bounded loads for dynamic environments [MTZ16]. It is concerned with designing consistent hashing schemes in dynamic environments that result in a pre-specified load balancing with a pre-specified maximum load on each machine, and a minimal number of movements. We show a new consistent hashing scheme with the idea of linear probing for which we can provably show its performance. The technique was adopted by the backend of Google cloud services and later on, by Vimeo video serving system. Another load balancing problems appears in the context of multi-dimensional dynamic load balancing [AMS$^+$17]. The third application is in online stochastic bin packing problems motivated by optimizing over-commitment in cloud services [CKMZ17].

Other than presenting theoretical results on these topics, we show how some of our new algorithmic techniques have been applied within the industry, and confirm their significance in practice. Throughout the talk, I focus on more recent results and present open problems.

3 BIOGRAPHY

Vahab Mirrokni is a principal scientist, heading the algorithms research groups at Google Research, New York. He received his PhD from MIT in 2005 and his B.Sc. from Sharif University of Technology in 2001. He joined Google Research in 2008, after spending a couple of years at Microsoft Research, MIT and Amazon.com. He is the co-winner of paper awards at KDD'15, ACM EC'08, and SODA'05. His research areas include algorithms, distributed and stochastic optimization, and computational economics. At Google, he is mainly working on algorithmic and economic problems related to search and online advertising. Recently he is working on online ad allocation problems, distributed algorithms for large-scale graph mining, and mechanism design for advertising exchanges.

REFERENCES

[AMS$^+$17] Aaron Archer, Vahab Mirrokni, Aaron Schild, Bartek Wydrowski, Ray Yang, and Morteza Zadimoghaddam. Dynamic load balancing for multiple dimensions. Working Paper, 2017.

[BBW13] Santiago R. Balseiro, Omar Besbes, and Gabriel Y. Weintraub. Auctions for online display advertising exchanges: Approximations and design. In *Proceedings of the Fourteenth ACM Conference on Electronic Commerce, EC '13*, pages 53–54. ACM, 2013.

[BKMM17] Santiago R. Balseiro, Anthony Kim, Mohammad Mahdian, and Vahab S. Mirrokni. Budget management strategies in repeated auctions. In *Proceedings of the 26th International Conference on World Wide Web, WWW 2017, Perth, Australia, April 3-7, 2017*, pages 15–23, 2017.

[BLM$^+$17] Santiago Balseiro, Max Lin, Vahab Mirrokni, Renato Paes Leme, Pingzhong Tang, and Song Zuo. Dynamic revenue sharing. 2017.

[BML17] Santiago R. Balseiro, Vahab S. Mirrokni, and Renato Paes Leme. Dynamic auctions with martingale utilities. In *Proceedings of the Eighteen ACM Conference on Economics and Computation, EC '17*, 2017.

[CKMZ17] Maxime C. Cohen, Philipp Keller, Vahab S. Mirrokni, and Morteza Zadimoghaddam. Overcommitment in cloud services - bin packing with chance constraints. In *SIGMetrics*, 2017.

[EKM15] Hossein Esfandiari, Nitish Korula, and Vahab S. Mirrokni. Online allocation with traffic spikes: Mixing adversarial and stochastic models. In *Proceedings of the Sixteenth ACM Conference on Economics and Computation, EC '15, Portland, OR, USA, June 15-19, 2015*, pages 169–186, 2015.

[FHK$^+$10] Jon Feldman, Monika Henzinger, Nitish Korula, Vahab S Mirrokni, and Cliff Stein. Online Stochastic Packing Applied to Display Ad Allocation. *ESA 2010*, pages 182–194, 2010.

[FKM$^+$09] Jon Feldman, Nitish Korula, Vahab Mirrokni, S. Muthukrishnan, and Martin Pál. Online ad assignment with free disposal. In *Proceedings of the 5th International Workshop on Internet and Network Economics, WINE '09*, pages 374–385. Springer-Verlag, 2009.

[GM14] Renato Gomes and Vahab S. Mirrokni. Optimal revenue-sharing double auctions with applications to ad exchanges. In *23rd International World Wide Web Conference, WWW '14, Seoul, Republic of Korea, April 7-11, 2014*, pages 19–28, 2014.

[KLN13] S. Kakade, I. Lobel, and H. Nazerzadeh. Optimal dynamic mechanism design and the virtual pivot mechanism. *Operations Research*, 61(3):837–854, 2013.

[KMN15] N. Korula, V. Mirrokni, and H. Nazerzadeh. Optimizing display advertising markets: Challenges and directions. forthcoming, *IEEE Internet Computing*, 2015.

[MGZ12] Vahab S. Mirrokni, Shayan Oveis Gharan, and Morteza Zadimoghaddam. Simultaneous approximations for adversarial and stochastic online budgeted allocation. In *Proceedings of the Twenty-Third Annual ACM-SIAM Symposium on Discrete Algorithms, SODA 2012, Kyoto, Japan, January 17-19, 2012*, pages 1690–1701, 2012.

[MLRZ17] Vahab Mirrokni, Renato Paes Leme, Rita Ren, and Song Zuo. Dynamic second price auctions with low regret. 2017.

[MLTZ16a] Vahab Mirrokni, Renato Paes Leme, Pingzhong Tang, and Song Zuo. Non-clairvoyant dynamic mechanism design. 2016.

[MLTZ16b] Vahab S. Mirrokni, Renato Paes Leme, Pingzhong Tang, and Song Zuo. Dynamic auctions with bank accounts. In *Proceedings of the Twenty-Fifth International Joint Conference on Artificial Intelligence, IJCAI 2016, New York, NY, USA, 9-15 July 2016*, pages 387–393, 2016.

[MN17] Vahab S. Mirrokni and Hamid Nazerzadeh. Deals or no deals: Contract design in onilne advertising. In *World Wide Web (WWW)*, pages 7–14, 2017.

[MTZ16] Vahab S. Mirrokni, Mikkel Thorup, and Morteza Zadimoghaddam. Consistent hashing with bounded loads. *CoRR*, abs/1608.01350, 2016.

Stein's Method for Mean-Field Approximations in Light and Heavy Traffic Regimes

Extended Abstract[*]

Lei Ying

School of Electrical, Computer and Energy Engineering, Arizona State University

Tempe, Arizona 85287

lei.ying.2@asu.edu

Mean-field analysis is an analytical method for understanding large-scale stochastic systems such as large-scale data centers and communication networks. The idea is to approximate the stationary distribution of a large-scale stochastic system using the equilibrium point (called the mean-field limit) of a dynamical system (called the mean-field model). This approximation is often justified by proving the weak convergence of stationary distributions to its mean-field limit. Most existing mean-field models concerned the light-traffic regime where the load of the system, denote by ρ, is strictly less than one and is independent of the size of the system. This is because a traditional mean-field model represents the limit of the corresponding stochastic system. Therefore, the load of the mean-field model is $\rho = \lim_{N\to\infty} \rho^{(N)}$, where $\rho^{(N)}$ is the load of the stochastic system of size N. Now if $\rho^{(N)} \to 1$ as $N \to \infty$ (i.e., in the heavy-traffic regime), then $\rho = 1$. For most systems, the mean-field limits when $\rho = 1$ are trivial and meaningless. To overcome this difficulty of traditional mean-field models, this paper takes a different point of view on mean-field models. Instead of regarding a mean-field model as the limiting system of large-scale stochastic system, it views the equilibrium point of the mean-field model, called a mean-field solution, simply as an approximation of the stationary distribution of the finite-size system. Therefore both mean-field models and solutions can be functions of N. The proposed method focuses on quantifying the approximation error. If the approximation error is small (as we will show in two applications), then we can conclude that the mean-field solution is a good approximation of the stationary distribution. The main results of this paper are summarized below.

Main Result 1: First, we outline the proposed approach, which synthesizes mean-field analysis, Stein's method and the perturbation theory. In particular, it is based on the following fundamental equation, which we call *Stein's equation for mean-field models*

$$E\left[d\left(X^{(N)}(\infty), x^{(N)*}\right)\right] = -E\left[\sum_y R_{X^{(N)}(\infty),y} \Gamma\left(X^{(N)}(\infty), y\right)\right],$$

where $X^{(N)}$ is a Continuous-Time-Markov-Chain (CTMC), $X^{(N)}(\infty)$ is its stationary distribution, $x^{(N)*}$ is the corresponding mean-field solution, $R_{x,y}$ is the transition rate of $X^{(N)}$ from state x to state y,

$$\Gamma(x, y) = g(y) - g(x) - \nabla g(x) \cdot (y - x),$$

and $g(x)$ is the solution of the Poisson equation and determined by the corresponding N-dependent mean-field model. When the closed-form expression of $g(x)$ is available, obtaining the error bound is straightforward. Otherwise, this paper presents a lemma based on the perturbation theory to bound $\Gamma(x, y)$.

Main Result 2: In the first application, we consider the $M/M/N$ queueing system (or Erlang-C queueing system), which consists of N servers and a single queue. For this system, the closed-form expression of $g(x)$ can be obtained. Assuming the arrival rate is λN, service times are exponential with mean 1, and $N(1 - \lambda) \geq 4$, we have

$$E\left[\left(\frac{Q^{(N)}(\infty)}{N} - \lambda\right)^2\right] \leq \frac{6(\lambda + 1)}{N} + \frac{36(1 + \lambda)}{N^2(1 - \lambda)^2},$$

where $Q^{(N)}(\infty)$ is the number of jobs in the system at the steady-state. This bound is *universal*. To see this, let $\lambda = 1 - \gamma N^{-\alpha}$, so $\gamma N^{1-\alpha}$ is the gap between the arrival rate and the total service rate. When α varies from 0 to 1, the gap $\gamma N^{1-\alpha}$ varies from a constant fraction of N (i.e., light load) to a constant independent of N (i.e., very heavy traffic load).

Main Result 3: In the second application, we consider the supermarket model under the-power-of-two-choices. Assuming $\lambda = 1 - \gamma N^{-\alpha}, 0 \leq \alpha < 0.2$, and an arbitrarily small $\xi' > 0$, the following inequality holds for sufficiently large N,

$$E\left[\sum_{k=0}^{\infty} \left|S_k^{(N)}(\infty) - s_k^{(N)*}\right|\right] \leq \frac{1}{N^{1-2\alpha-\xi'}},$$

where $S_k^{(N)}(\infty)$ is the number of servers with queue size at least k at the steady-state, and $s_k^{(N)*} = (1 - \gamma N^{-\alpha})^{2^k - 1}$. We remark that this is the first result that quantifies the steady-state performance of the-power-of-two-choices in the heavy traffic regime.

ACKNOWLEDGEMENT

The author sincerely thank Jim Dai for the numerous discussions that motivated this work and inspired many results in this paper. The author also thank R. Srikant for his invaluable comments and feedback. This work was supported in part by NSF Grants CNS-1262329, ECCS-1547294, ECCS-1609202, and the U.S. Office of Naval Research (ONR Grant No. N00014-15-1-2169).

---

[*] The full version of this paper is available at inlab.lab.asu.edu/Publications/stein-mf.pdf.

SIGMETRICS '17, June 5–9, 2017, Urbana-Champaign, IL, USA
© 2017 Copyright held by the owner/author(s). ACM ISBN 978-1-4503-5032-7/17/06.
DOI: http://dx.doi.org/10.1145/3078505.3078592

Expected Values Estimated via Mean-Field Approximation are 1/N-Accurate

Extended Abstract*

Nicolas Gast

Inria

Univ. Grenoble Alpes, CNRS, LIG

Grenoble, France F-38000

nicolas.gast@inria.fr

ABSTRACT

In this paper, we study the accuracy of mean-field approximation. We show that, under general conditions, the expectation of any performance functional converges at rate $O(1/N)$ to its mean-field approximation. Our result applies for finite and infinite-dimensional mean-field models. We provide numerical experiments that demonstrate that this rate of convergence is tight.

CCS CONCEPTS

• **General and reference** → **Performance**; • **Mathematics of computing** → **Stochastic processes**; *Queueing theory*; Ordinary differential equations;

KEYWORDS

Mean-field approximation; queueing theory; accuracy of approximation; supermarket model; power-of-two-choice

ACM Reference format:
Nicolas Gast. 2017. Expected Values Estimated via Mean-Field Approximation are 1/N-Accurate. In *Proceedings of SIGMETRICS '17, Urbana-Champaign, IL, USA, June 05-09, 2017,* 1 pages.
https://doi.org/10.1145/3078505.3078523

1 INTRODUCTION

Mean-field approximation is a powerful tool for studying systems composed of a large number of interacting objects. The idea of mean-field approximation is to replace a complex stochastic system by a simpler deterministic dynamical system. This approximation is widely used to study the performance of computer-based systems. This approximation is known to be asymptotically exact for many systems, in which the fraction of objects in a given state i, $X_i^{(N)}$, converges at rate $O(1/\sqrt{N})$ to a deterministic quantity x_i, as the number of objects N goes to infinity [2, 5].

In this paper, we show that, when one wants to estimate expected values, the rate of convergence is much faster. More precisely, we

*Full version of the paper : https://github.com/ngast/meanFieldAccuracy [1].

show that for a smooth function h, the expectation $\mathbb{E}[h(X^{(N)})]$ converges at rate $1/N$ to its mean-field approximation $h(x)$:

$$\left| \mathbb{E}\left[h(X^{(N)}) \right] - h(x) \right| = O\left(\frac{1}{N} \right). \quad (1)$$

We show that this essentially holds for the transient regime as soon as the drift of the system is twice-differentiable. It holds for the stationary regime if in addition the differential equation has a unique stable point that is exponentially stable. We also exhibit an example that shows that when the drift of the system is only Lipschitz-continuous, the convergence can be slower.

As an example, we study in detail the convergence rate of the classical power-of-two-choice model (*a.k.a.* supermarket model) of [3, 4]. These papers show that, as the number of servers N go to infinity, the average queue length goes to $m^\infty(\rho) = \Theta(\log 1/(1-\rho))$.

Our results show that an average value estimated via mean-field approximation is 1/N-accurate. In a queuing network such as the two-choice model, the average queue length can be expressed as $\mathbb{E}[h(X^{(N)})]$. Equation (1) shows that the average queue length converges at rate $O(1/N)$ to its mean-field approximation. We provide numerical evidence that for this model, for any finite value of N, the average queue length is $m^N(\rho) \approx m^\infty(\rho) + \frac{\rho^2}{2N(1-\rho)}$. We illustrate this in Table 1 where we report the average queue length for $\rho = 0.9$. We observe that $m^N(0.9) \approx m^\infty(0.9) + 4/N$.

Number of servers (N)	10	100	1000	$+\infty$
Average queue length (m^N)	2.81	2.39	2.36	2.35
Error ($m^N - m^\infty$)	0.45	0.039	0.004	0

Table 1: Average queue length for the two-choice model.

REFERENCES

[1] Nicolas Gast. 2017. Expected values estimated via mean-field approximation are 1/N-accurate. In *Proceedings of the 2017 ACM SIGMETRICS*. ACM. https://github.com/ngast/meanFieldAccuracy

[2] Thomas G Kurtz. 1970. Solutions of Ordinary Differential Equations as Limits of Pure Jump Markov Processes. *Journal of Applied Probability* 7 (1970), 49–58.

[3] Michael David Mitzenmacher. 1996. *The Power of Two Random Choices in Randomized Load Balancing.* Ph.D. Dissertation. PhD thesis, Graduate Division of the University of California at Berkley.

[4] Nikita Dmitrievna Vvedenskaya, Roland L'vovich Dobrushin, and Fridrikh Izrailevich Karpelevich. 1996. Queueing system with selection of the shortest of two queues: An asymptotic approach. *Problemy Peredachi Informatsii* 32, 1 (1996), 20–34.

[5] Lei Ying. 2016. On the Approximation Error of Mean-Field Models. In *Proceedings of the 2016 ACM SIGMETRICS International Conference on Measurement and Modeling of Computer Science.* ACM, 285–297.

Analysis of a Stochastic Model of Replication in Large Distributed Storage Systems: A Mean-Field Approach

Wen Sun
INRIA
Paris F-75012, France
Wen.Sun@inria.fr

Véronique Simon
Sorbonne Universités & UPMC
Paris 75005, France
vsimon19@gmail.com

Sébastien Monnet
LISTIC - Polytech Annecy-Chambéry
Annecy le Vieux 74944, France
Sebastien.Monnet@univ-smb.fr

Philippe Robert
INRIA
Paris F-75012, France
Philippe.Robert@inria.fr

Pierre Sens
Sorbonne Universités & UPMC
Paris 75005, France
Pierre.Sens@lip6.fr

ABSTRACT

Distributed storage systems such as Hadoop File System or Google File System (GFS) ensure data availability and durability using replication. Persistence is achieved by replicating the same data block on several nodes, and ensuring that a minimum number of copies are available on the system at any time. Whenever the contents of a node are lost, for instance due to a hard disk crash, the system regenerates the data blocks stored before the failure by transferring them from the remaining replicas. This paper is focused on the analysis of the efficiency of replication mechanism that determines the location of the copies of a given file at some server. The variability of the loads of the nodes of the network is investigated for several policies. Three replication mechanisms are tested against simulations in the context of a real implementation of a such a system: Random, Least Loaded and Power of Choice.

The simulations show that some of these policies may lead to quite unbalanced situations: if β is the average number of copies per node it turns out that, at equilibrium, the load of the nodes may exhibit a high variability. It is shown in this paper that a simple variant of a power of choice type algorithm has a striking effect on the loads of the nodes: at equilibrium, the distribution of the load of a node has a bounded support, most of nodes have a load less than 2β which is an interesting property for the design of the storage space of these systems. Stochastic models are introduced and investigated to explain this interesting phenomenon. Arxiv URL of the full paper.

CCS CONCEPTS

• **Computer systems organization** → **Reliability**; • **Mathematics of computing** → *Stochastic processes*; • **Networks** → *Network performance modeling*;

KEYWORDS

Placement Algorithms; Stochastic Models; DHT; Performance

SIGMETRICS '17, June 5-9, 2017, *Urbana-Champaign, IL, USA*
© 2017 Copyright held by the owner/author(s). 978-1-4503-5032-7/17/06.
DOI: http://dx.doi.org/10.1145/3078505.3078531

ACM Reference format:
Wen Sun, Véronique Simon, Sébastien Monnet, Philippe Robert, and Pierre Sens. 2017. Analysis of a Stochastic Model of Replication in Large Distributed Storage Systems: A Mean-Field Approach. In *Proceedings of SIGMETRICS '17, Urbana-Champaign,IL, USA, June 05-09, 2017*, 1 pages.
DOI: http://dx.doi.org/10.1145/3078505.3078531

MAIN RESULTS

In this paper we study data placement policies avoiding data redistribution: once a piece of data is assigned to a node, it will remain on it until the node crashes. We focus specifically on the evaluation of the impact of several placement strategies on the storage load balance on a long term. Our investigation has been done in two complementary steps.

(1) A simulation environment of a real system based on PeerSim is used to emulate several years of evolution of this system for three placement policies which are defined below: Random, Least Loaded and Power of Choice.

(2) Simplified mathematical models are presented to analyze the Random and Power of Choice Policies. Mean-field results are obtained when the number N of nodes gets large.

We show that, for a large network with an average load β per node, if $\overline{X}_\beta^R$, [resp. $\overline{X}_\beta^P$] is the load of a random node at equilibrium for the Random policy [resp. Power of choice policy] then, for $x \geq 0$,

$$\lim_{\beta \to +\infty} \mathbb{P}\left(\overline{X}_\beta^R/\beta \geq x\right) = e^{-x},$$

$$\lim_{\beta \to +\infty} \mathbb{P}\left(\overline{X}_\beta^P/\beta \geq x\right) = \begin{cases} 1 - x/2 & \text{if } x < 2, \\ 0 & \text{if } x \geq 2. \end{cases}$$

The striking feature is that, for the Power of choice policy and for a large average load per node β, the distribution of the load of a node has, asymptotically, the *finite support* $[0, 2\beta]$. This is an important and desirable property for the design of such systems, to dimension the storage of the nodes in particular. Note that this is not the case for the Random policy. Our simulations of a real system exhibit this surprising phenomenon, even for moderately large loads.

Understanding Reduced-Voltage Operation in Modern DRAM Devices:
Experimental Characterization, Analysis, and Mechanisms[*]

Kevin K. Chang[†]   Abdullah Giray Yağlıkçı[†]   Saugata Ghose[†]   Aditya Agrawal[¶]   Niladrish Chatterjee[¶]

Abhijith Kashyap[¶]   Donghyuk Lee[¶]   Mike O'Connor[¶,‡]   Hasan Hassan[§]   Onur Mutlu[§,†]

[†]Carnegie Mellon University   [¶]NVIDIA   [‡]The University of Texas at Austin   [§]ETH Zürich

ABSTRACT

The energy consumption of DRAM is a critical concern in modern computing systems. Improvements in manufacturing process technology have allowed DRAM vendors to lower the DRAM supply voltage conservatively, which reduces some of the DRAM energy consumption. We would like to reduce the DRAM supply voltage more aggressively, to further reduce energy. Aggressive supply voltage reduction requires a thorough understanding of the effect voltage scaling has on DRAM access latency and DRAM reliability.

In this paper, we take a comprehensive approach to understanding and exploiting the latency and reliability characteristics of modern DRAM when the supply voltage is lowered below the nominal voltage level specified by manufacturers. Using an FPGA-based testing platform, we perform an experimental study of 124 real DDR3L (low-voltage) DRAM chips manufactured recently by three major DRAM vendors. Our extensive experimental characterization yields four major observations on how DRAM latency, reliability, and data retention are affected by reduced voltage.

First, we observe that we can reliably access data when DRAM supply voltage is lowered below the nominal voltage level, *until a certain voltage value*, V_{min}, which is the minimum voltage level at which no bit errors occur. Furthermore, we find that we can reduce the voltage below V_{min} to attain further energy savings, but that errors start occurring in some of the data read from memory. As we drop the voltage further below V_{min}, the number of erroneous bits of data increases exponentially.

Second, we observe that while reducing the voltage below V_{min} introduces bit errors in the data, we can prevent these errors if we increase the latency of three major DRAM operations, i.e., activation, restoration, and precharge. When the supply voltage is reduced, the DRAM cell capacitor charge takes a longer time to change, thereby causing these DRAM operations to become slower to complete. Errors are introduced into the data when the memory controller does *not* account for this slowdown in the DRAM operations. We find that if the memory controller allocates extra time for these operations to finish when the supply voltage is below V_{min}, errors no longer occur. We validate, analyze, and explain this behavior using detailed circuit-level simulations.

Third, we observe that when only a small number of errors occur due to reduced supply voltage, these errors tend to *cluster* physically in certain *regions* of a DRAM chip, as opposed to being randomly distributed throughout the chip. This observation implies that when we reduce the supply voltage to the DRAM array, we need to increase the fundamental operation latencies for *only* the regions where errors can occur.

Fourth, we observe that reducing the supply voltage does *not* affect the data retention guarantees of DRAM. Commodity DRAM chips guarantee that all cells can safely retain data for 64ms, after which the cells are *refreshed* to replenish charge that leaks out of the capacitors. Even when we reduce the supply voltage, the rate at which charge leaks from the capacitors is so slow that no data is lost during the 64ms refresh interval at both 20℃ and 70℃.

Based on our observations, we propose a new DRAM energy reduction mechanism, called *Voltron*. The key idea of Voltron is to use a performance model to determine by how much we can reduce the supply voltage without introducing errors and without exceeding a user-specified threshold for performance loss. Unlike prior works, Voltron does *not* reduce the voltage of the *peripheral circuitry*, which is responsible for transferring commands and data between the memory controller and the DRAM chip. If Voltron were to reduce the voltage of the peripheral circuitry, we would have to reduce the operating frequency of DRAM. A reduction in the operating frequency reduces the memory data throughput, which can significantly degrade the performance of applications that require high memory bandwidth. Our evaluations show that Voltron reduces the average DRAM and system energy consumption by 10.5% and 7.3%, respectively, while limiting the average system performance loss to only 1.8%, for a variety of memory-intensive quad-core workloads. We also show that Voltron significantly outperforms prior dynamic voltage and frequency scaling mechanisms for DRAM.

KEYWORDS

DRAM; Voltage Reduction; Memory Latency; Reliability; Performance; Energy; DRAM Characterization; Memory Systems

ACM Reference format:
Kevin K. Chang, Abdullah Giray Yağlıkçı, Saugata Ghose, Aditya Agrawal, Niladrish Chatterjee, Abhijith Kashyap, Donghyuk Lee, Mike O'Connor, Hasan Hassan, and Onur Mutlu. 2017. Understanding Reduced-Voltage Operation in Modern DRAM Devices: Experimental Characterization, Analysis, and Mechanisms. In *Proceedings of SIGMETRICS '17, June 5–9, 2017, Urbana-Champaign, IL, USA*, 1 pages.
DOI: http://dx.doi.org/10.1145/3078505.3078590

[*]The full version of the paper is available at http://www.ece.cmu.edu/~safari/pubs.html

Exploiting Data Longevity for Enhancing the Lifetime of Flash-based Storage Class Memory

Wonil Choi †   Mohammad Arjomand †   Myoungsoo Jung ‡   Mahmut T. Kandemir †

† Pennsylvania State University   ‡ Yonsei University

ABSTRACT

This paper proposes to exploit the capability of retention time relaxation in flash memories for improving the lifetime of an SLC-based SSD. The main idea is that as a majority of I/O data in a typical workload do not need a retention time larger than a few days, we can have multiple partial program states in a cell and use every two states to store one-bit data at each time. Thus, we can store multiple bits in a cell (one bit at each time) without erasing it after each write – that would directly translate into lifetime enhancement. The proposed scheme is called Dense-SLC (D-SLC) flash design which improves SSD lifetime by 5.1×–8.6×.

ACM Reference format:
Wonil Choi †   Mohammad Arjomand †   Myoungsoo Jung ‡   Mahmut T. Kandemir †. 2017. Exploiting Data Longevity for Enhancing the Lifetime of Flash-based Storage Class Memory. In *Proceedings of SIGMETRICS '17, Urbana-Champaign, IL, USA, June 05-09, 2017,* 1 pages.
https://doi.org/http://dx.doi.org/10.1145/3078505.3078527

1 DENSE-SLC NAND FLASH-BASED SSD

A typical flash-based Storage Class Memory (SCM) has a hierarchal internal structure: there is a fast Single-Level Cell (SLC) Solid State Drive (SSD) with tens of gigabytes capacity at the upper level and a slow Multi-Level Cell (MLC) SSD with terabyte capacity at the lower level. In this setup, the SLC SSD services a great portion of the incoming traffic which poses high write pressure on it – this makes write endurance a significant challenge for the SLC SSD part (each flash cell can tolerate 10^4–10^5 program/erase cycles). This paper targets the lifetime problem of SLC SSD and discusses the opportunity for improving it by relaxing its *retention time*.

Motivation – The flash devices are traditionally expected to retain data for one or more years. However, the stored data in an SSD SCM does *not* require this long-term non-volatility. Within a hierarchical SCM, we expect the SLC SSD to handle the I/O requests with short-term longevity, while the I/O requests with long-term longevity are normally handled by the underlying MLC SSD. As a motivation example, Figure 1 (left) shows the CDF of data longevity for I/O data in mds_0. We can see that more than 90% of written data in mds_0 have a longevity of up to 10 hours. Similar behaviors were observed for a wide range of enterprise workloads.

Proposal – The main idea is that, by relaxing the retention time of an SLC device, we can have more than two states in a cell. At each given time, similar to the conventional SLC, we use every

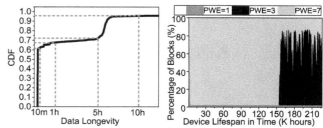

Figure 1: Data longevity and PWE analysis for mds_0.

two states to write one bit information. In this way, a device stores multiple bits (one bit at each time) before it needs an erase, thereby increasing the number writes to cell during one erase cycle, or increasing the maximum number of *logical pages* stored in *one physical page* during *one P/E cycle* (we call this "page writes per erase cycle" or PWE, i.e., always one in the conventional SLC flash). Clearly, increasing PWE leads to device lifetime improvement.

We propose Dense-SLC (D-SLC) flash where each flash block has one of the three modes: all pages/cells in it are in 2-state mode (same as the conventional SLC), 4-state mode (it has two intermediate states; its PWE is three), or 8-state mode (it has 6 intermediate states; its PWE is 7). An 8-state mode block has the shortest retention time and suitable for storing data with short longevity (e.g., less than an hour), whereas a 2-state mode block has the longest retention time and suitable for data with long longevity (e.g., greater than 3 days). The 4-state mode has a moderate retention time and is used for data with "10 hours to 3 days longevity".

Results – We used Disksim with the SSD extensions by Microsoft to model an SLC SSD for our evaluation. Figure 1 (right) shows the percentages of blocks with 2, 4, and 8 states for mds_0 during the entire device lifetime – this shows that our proposed flash can store more I/O data by storing them into 4 and 8-state mode blocks (compared to the conventional SLC with 2-state mode blocks only). For the 15 evaluated workloads from MSR Cambridge suite, our D-SLC design improves the device lifetime by 5.1×–8.6×.

D-SLC in detail – D-SLC implementation requires hardware/software supports, including calibrating the parameters of the flash programming algorithm and modifying block selection and garbage collection algorithms at flash software (FTL). Detailed description and analysis of the D-SLC design are available at [1].

2 ACKNOWLEDGMENT

This work is supported in part by NSF grants 1302557, 1213052, 1439021, 1302225, 1629129, 1526750, and 1629915, a grant from Intel, NRF 2016R1C1B2015312 and 2015M3C4A7065645, and MSIP IITP-2015-R0346-15-1008.

REFERENCES

[1] Wonil Choi, Mohammad Arjomand, Myoungsoo Jung, and Mahmut T. Kandemir. 2017. Exploiting Data Longevity for Enhancing the Lifetime of Flash-based Storage Class Memory. In *SIGMETRICS*. https://arxiv.org/abs/1704.05138.

Design-Induced Latency Variation in Modern DRAM Chips: Characterization, Analysis, and Latency Reduction Mechanisms*

Donghyuk Lee[†‡]   Samira Khan[※]   Lavanya Subramanian[†]   Saugata Ghose[†]

Rachata Ausavarungnirun[†]   Gennady Pekhimenko[†¶]   Vivek Seshadri[†¶]   Onur Mutlu[†§]

[†]*Carnegie Mellon University*   [‡]*NVIDIA*   [※]*University of Virginia*   [¶]*Microsoft Research*   [§]*ETH Zürich*

ABSTRACT

Variation has been shown to exist across the cells within a modern DRAM chip. Prior work has studied and exploited several forms of variation, such as manufacturing-process- or temperature-induced variation. We empirically demonstrate a new form of variation that exists within a real DRAM chip, *induced by the design and placement* of different components in the DRAM chip: different regions in DRAM, based on their relative distances from the peripheral structures, require different minimum access latencies for reliable operation. In particular, we show that in most real DRAM chips, cells closer to the peripheral structures can be accessed much faster than cells that are farther. We call this phenomenon *design-induced variation in DRAM*. Our goals are to *i)* understand design-induced variation that exists in real, state-of-the-art DRAM chips, *ii)* exploit it to develop low-cost mechanisms that can dynamically find and use the *lowest latency at which to operate a DRAM chip reliably*, and, thus, *iii)* improve overall system performance while ensuring reliable system operation.

To this end, we first experimentally demonstrate and analyze designed-induced variation in modern DRAM devices by testing and characterizing 96 DIMMs (768 DRAM chips). Our experimental study shows that *i)* modern DRAM chips exhibit design-induced latency variation in both row and column directions, *ii)* access latency gradually increases in the row direction within a DRAM cell array (mat) and this pattern repeats in every mat, and *iii)* some columns require higher latency than others due to the internal hierarchical organization of the DRAM chip.

Our characterization identifies DRAM regions that are *vulnerable* to errors, if operated at lower latency, and finds consistency in their locations across a given DRAM chip generation, due to design-induced variation. Variations in the vertical and horizontal dimensions, together, divide the cell array into heterogeneous-latency regions, where cells in some regions require longer access latencies for reliable operation. Reducing the latency *uniformly across all*

regions in DRAM would improve performance, but can introduce failures in the *inherently slower* regions that require longer access latencies for correct operation. We refer to these inherently slower regions of DRAM as design-induced *vulnerable regions*.

Based on our extensive experimental analysis, we develop two mechanisms that reliably reduce DRAM latency. First, DIVA Profiling uses runtime profiling to *dynamically* identify the lowest DRAM latency that does not introduce failures. DIVA Profiling exploits design-induced variation and periodically profiles *only* the *vulnerable regions* to determine the lowest DRAM latency at low cost. It is the first mechanism to *dynamically* determine the lowest latency that can be used to operate DRAM *reliably*. DIVA Profiling reduces the latency of read/write requests by 35.1%/57.8%, respectively, at 55°C. Our second mechanism, DIVA Shuffling, shuffles data such that values stored in vulnerable regions are mapped to multiple error-correcting code (ECC) codewords. As a result, DIVA Shuffling can correct 26% more multi-bit errors than conventional ECC. Combined together, our two mechanisms reduce read/write latency by 40.0%/60.5%, which translates to an overall system performance improvement of 14.7%/13.7%/13.8% (in 2-/4-/8-core systems) over a variety of workloads, while ensuring reliable operation.

CCS CONCEPTS

• **Computer systems organization → Architectures; Processors and memory architectures; Reliability;** • **Hardware → Dynamic memory;**

KEYWORDS

Memory Systems; DRAM; Latency Variation; Fault Tolerance

ACM Reference format:
Donghyuk Lee, Samira Khan, Lavanya Subramanian, Saugata Ghose, Rachata Ausavarungnirun, Gennady Pekhimenko, Vivek Seshadri, and Onur Mutlu. 2017. Design-Induced Latency Variation in Modern DRAM Chips: Characterization, Analysis, and Latency Reduction Mechanisms. In *Proceedings of SIGMETRICS '17, June 5–9, 2017, Urbana-Champaign, IL, USA,* 1 page.
DOI: http://dx.doi.org/10.1145/3078505.3078533

---

*The full version of the paper is available at http://www.ece.cmu.edu/~safari/pubs.html

---

Hadoop on Named Data Networking:
Experience and Results

Mathias Gibbens
Chris Gniady
Lei Ye
Beichuan Zhang
The University of Arizona
Department of Computer Science
Tucson, AZ 85721, USA

ABSTRACT

In today's data centers, clusters of servers are arranged to perform various tasks in a massively distributed manner: handling web requests, processing scientific data, and running simulations of real-world problems. These clusters are very complex, and require a significant amount of planning and administration to ensure that they perform to their maximum potential. Planning and configuration can be a long and complicated process; once completed it is hard to completely re-architect an existing cluster. In addition to planning the physical hardware, the software must also be properly configured to run on a cluster. Information such as which server is in which rack and the total network bandwidth between rows of racks constrain the placement of jobs scheduled to run on a cluster. Some software may be able to use hints provided by a user about where to schedule jobs, while others may simply place them randomly and hope for the best.

Every cluster has at least one bottleneck that constrains the overall performance to less than the optimal that may be achieved on paper. One common bottleneck is the speed of the network: communication between servers in a rack may be unable to saturate their network connections, but traffic flowing between racks or rows in a data center can easily overwhelm the interconnect switches. Various network topologies have been proposed to help mitigate this problem by providing multiple paths between points in the network, but they all suffer from the same fundamental problem: it is cost-prohibitive to build a network that can provide concurrent full network bandwidth between all servers. Researchers have been working on developing new network protocols that can make more efficient use of existing network hardware through a blurring of the line between network layer and applications. One of the most well-known examples of this is Named Data Networking (NDN), a data-centric network architecture that has been in development for several years.

While NDN has received significant attention for wide-area Internet, a detailed understanding of NDN benefits and challenges in the data center environment has been lacking. The Named Data Networking architecture retrieves content by names rather than connecting to specific hosts. It provides benefits such as highly efficient and resilient content distribution, which fit well to data-intensive distributed computing. This paper presents and discusses our experience in modifying Apache Hadoop, a popular MapReduce framework, to operate on an NDN network. Through this first-of-its-kind implementation process, we demonstrate the feasibility of running an existing, large, and complex piece of distributed software commonly seen in data centers over NDN. We show advantages such as simplified network code and reduced network traffic, which are beneficial in a data center environment. There are also challenges faced by NDN that are being addressed by the community, which can be magnified under data center traffic. Through detailed evaluation, we show a reduction of 16% for overall data transmission between Hadoop nodes while writing data with default replication settings. Preliminary results also show promise for in-network caching of repeated reads in distributed applications. We show that while overall performance is currently slower under NDN, there are challenges and opportunities for further NDN improvements.

Link to full draft of paper:
https://www2.cs.arizona.edu/people/gibmat/papers/ sigmetrics17.pdf

KEYWORDS

Named Data Networking; Large-scale systems; Hadoop; Data centers; Emerging technologies

ACM Reference format:
Mathias Gibbens, Chris Gniady, Lei Ye, and Beichuan Zhang. 2017. Hadoop on Named Data Networking: Experience and Results. In *Proceedings of SIGMETRICS '17, June 5-9, 2017, Urbana-Champaign, IL, USA, , 1 pages.*
DOI: http://dx.doi.org/10.1145/3078505.3078508

Using Burstable Instances in the Public Cloud: Why, When and How?*

Cheng Wang, Bhuvan Urgaonkar, Neda Nasiriani, George Kesidis[†]

School of EECS, Penn State University

cxw967,buu1,nun129,gik2@psu.edu

CCS CONCEPTS

Computer systems organization   *Cloud computing*;

KEYWORDS

Burstable instance; capacity dynamism; resource allocation

ACM Reference format:
Cheng Wang, Bhuvan Urgaonkar, Neda Nasiriani, George Kesidis.
2017. Using Burstable Instances in the Public Cloud: Why, When
and How?. In *Proceedings of SIGMETRICS '17, June 5–9, 2017,
Urbana-Champaign, IL, USA, ,* 1 pages.
https://doi.org/http://dx.doi.org/10.1145/3078505.3078591

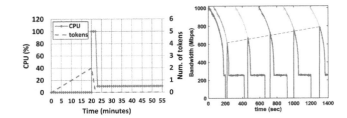

Figure 1: The token-bucket mechanisms of the CPU capacity and network bandwidth for Amazon EC2's t2.micro.

1 INTRODUCTION

Type	Resource capacity	Disclosure	Examples from EC2 and GCE instance offerings
1	Fixed	Full	main memory capacity and CPU cycles (except for burstables); most resources for larger instances
2A	Random w/ low variance	Partial or full	network and memory b/w for larger regular instances
2B	Random w/ high variance	Partial or full	network and memory b/w for smaller instances (including for burstables)
3A	Deterministic	Full	token-bucket regulated CPU for EC2's burstables; remote disk b/w for both regular and burstable instances from both EC2 and GCE
3B	Deterministic	None or partial	token-bucket regulated CPU for GCE burstable instances; network b/w for EC2's burstable instances

Table 1: Our classification of resource capacity dynamism for GCE and EC2 instances along with the nature of disclosure made by the provider.

To attract more customers, public cloud providers offer virtual machine (instance) types that trade off lower prices for poorer capacities. As one salient approach, the providers employ *aggressive statistical multiplexing* of multiple cheaper instances on a single physical server, resulting in tenants experiencing higher dynamism in the resource capacity of these instances. Examples of this are EC2's "t type" instances and

GCE's "shared-core" instances. We collectively refer to these as burstable instances for their ability to dynamically "burst" (increase the capacity of) their resources.

Burstable instances are significantly cheaper than the "regular" instances, and offer time-varying CPU capacity comprising a minimum guaranteed base capacity/rate, which is much smaller than a short-lived peak capacity that becomes available upon operating at lower than base rate for a sufficient duration. Table 1 summarizes our classification of resource capacity dynamism for GCE and EC2 instances along with the nature of disclosure made by the provider. To exploit burstable instances cost-effectively, a tenant would need to carefully understand the *significant additional complexity* of such instances beyond that disclosed by the providers.

2 BURSTABLE INFERENCE AND USE

Although the resource capacities of burstables are variable, they are *not* random. In fact, we find that the CPU capacity and network bandwidth follow deterministic token-bucket regulation mechanisms which the tenant can leverage by adjusting its usage patterns (Figure 1). However, we find different levels of disclosure from EC2: whereas the CPU token bucket parameters are described, the network bandwidth regulation mechanism needs to be inferred by the tenant.

In the full version of our paper, we present analytical models for these regulation mechanisms. To demonstrate how tenants could use these models to exploit burstable instances cost-effectively, we present two case studies, both based on memcached. (i) Augmenting cheap but low availability EC2 spot instances with passive backup of popular content on burstable instances may offer improved failure recovery (with lower performance degradation) than using regular instances for such backup. (ii) Temporal multiplexing of multiple burstable instances may allow us to achieve the CPU or network bandwidth equivalent of a regular EC2 instance at 25% lower cost.

*The full version is available at http://www.cse.psu.edu/~bhuvan/papers/ps/sigmetrics17-burstables.pdf

[†]The authors have been listed in a reverse-alphabetical order of their last names.

SIGMETRICS '17, , June 5–9, 2017, Urbana-Champaign, IL, USA
© 2017 Copyright held by the owner/author(s).
ACM ISBN ACM ISBN 978-1-4503-5032-7/17/06.
https://doi.org/http://dx.doi.org/10.1145/3078505.3078591

Dandelion: Redesigning the Bitcoin Network for Anonymity

Shaileshh Bojja
Venkatakrishnan
University of Illinois at
Urbana-Champaign
bjjvnkt2@illinois.edu

Giulia Fanti
University of Illinois at
Urbana-Champaign
fanti@illinois.edu

Pramod Viswanath
University of Illinois at
Urbana-Champaign
pramodv@illinois.edu

ACM Reference format:
Shaileshh Bojja Venkatakrishnan, Giulia Fanti, and Pramod Viswanath. 2017.
Dandelion: Redesigning the Bitcoin Network for Anonymity. In *Proceedings
of SIGMETRICS '17, June 5–9, 2017, Urbana-Champaign, IL, USA, ,* 1 pages.
DOI: http://dx.doi.org/10.1145/3078505.3078528

Cryptocurrencies are digital currencies that provide cryptographic verification of transactions. In recent years, they have transitioned from an academic research topic to a multi-billion dollar industry [2]. Bitcoin is the best-known example of a cryptocurrency [3].

Cryptocurrencies exhibit two key properties: egalitarianism and transparency. In this context, *egalitarianism* means that no single party wields disproportionate power over the network's operation. This diffusion of power is achieved by asking other network nodes (e.g., other Bitcoin users) to validate transactions, instead of the traditional method of using a centralized authority for this purpose. Moreover, all transactions and communications are managed over a fully-distributed, peer-to-peer (P2P) network. Cryptocurrencies are *transparent* in the sense that all transactions are verified and recorded with cryptographic integrity guarantees; this prevents fraudulent activity like double-spending of money. Transparency is achieved through a combination of clever cryptographic protocols and the publication of transactions in a ledger known as a *blockchain*. This blockchain serves as a public record of every financial transaction in the network.

A property that Bitcoin does *not* provide is anonymity. Each user is identified in the network by a public, cryptographic key. If one were to link such a key to its owner's human identity, the owner's financial history could be partially learned from the public blockchain. In practice, it is possible to link public keys to identities through a number of channels, including the networking protocols on which Bitcoin is built [1]. This is a massive privacy violation, and can be dangerous for deanonymized users.

The objective of this paper is to redesign the Bitcoin networking stack from *first principles* to *prevent network-facilitated deanonymization* of users. Critically, this redesign must not reduce the network's reliability or performance. Although the networking stack is only one avenue for deanonymization attacks, it is an avenue that is powerful, poorly-understood, and often-ignored.

We seek a network management policy that exhibits two properties: (a) strong anonymity against an adversarial group of colluding nodes (which are a fraction p of the total network size), and (b) low broadcasting latency. The anonymity guarantees we provide are network-wide, uniformly protecting all users against a full-network deanonymization. Critically, these networking protocols should be *lightweight* and provide *statistical anonymity guarantees against computationally-unbounded adversaries*. Part of the novelty of our work is that the Bitcoin P2P networking stack has not been modeled in any detailed way (much less analyzed theoretically), to the best of our knowledge. In addition to modeling this complex, real-world networking system, our contributions are threefold:

(1) Fundamental anonymity bounds. The act of user deanonymization can be thought of as classifying transactions to source nodes. Hence we use precision and recall as natural performance metrics. Given a networking protocol, the adversary has a region of feasible (recall, precision) operating points, which are achieved by varying the source classification algorithm. We give fundamental bounds on the best precision and recall achieved by the adversary for any networking protocol.

(2) Optimal algorithm. We propose a simple networking protocol called DANDELION, whose achievable precision-recall region is nearly optimal, in the sense that it is contained in the achievable region of (nearly) every other possible networking protocol. DANDELION consists of two phases. In the first phase, each transaction is propagated on a random line; that is, each relay passes the message to exactly one (random) node for a random number of hops. In the second phase, the message is broadcast as fast as possible using diffusion. DANDELION has two key features: (a) in the first phase, all transactions from all sources should propagate over the *same* line, and (b) the adversary should not be able to learn the structure of the line beyond the adversarial nodes' immediate neighbors.

(3) Practical considerations. We outline the practical challenges associated with implementing DANDELION. In particular, constructing the graph for DANDELION in a distributed fashion, and enforcing the assumption that the adversary cannot learn the graph, are non-trivial. We therefore propose simple heuristics for addressing these challenges. A preprint of our full-paper can be found at [4].

REFERENCES

[1] Alex Biryukov, Dmitry Khovratovich, and Ivan Pustogarov. 2014. Deanonymisation of clients in Bitcoin P2P network. In *Proceedings of the 2014 ACM SIGSAC Conference on Computer and Communications Security*. ACM, 15–29.
[2] CoinMarketCap. 2016. Cryptocurrency Market Capitalizations. (2016).
[3] Satoshi Nakamoto. 2008. Bitcoin: A peer-to-peer electronic cash system. (2008).
[4] Shaileshh Bojja Venkatakrishnan, Giulia Fanti, and Pramod Viswanath. 2017. Dandelion: Redesigning the Bitcoin Network for Anonymity. *arXiv preprint arXiv:1701.04439* (2017).

On Gradient-Based Optimization: Accelerated, Distributed, Asynchronous and Stochastic

SIGMETRICS 2017 Keynote Talk

Michael J. Jordan
University of California, Berkeley

ABSTRACT

Many new theoretical challenges have arisen in the area of gradient-based optimization for large-scale statistical data analysis, driven by the needs of applications and the opportunities provided by new hardware and software platforms. I discuss several recent results in this area, including: (1) a new framework for understanding Nesterov acceleration, obtained by taking a continuous-time, Lagrangian/Hamiltonian perspective, (2) a general theory of asynchronous optimization in multi-processor systems, (3) a computationally-efficient approach to stochastic variance reduction, (4) a primal-dual methodology for gradient-based optimization that targets communication bottlenecks in distributed systems, and (5) a discussion of how to avoid saddle-points in nonconvex optimization.

CCS CONCEPTS

• **Theory of computation → Design and analysis of algorithms**; *Mathematical Optimization*→ Continuous optimization; **Theory and algorithms for application domains**; *Mathematical Optimization*→ Machine learning theory

KEYWORDS

Gradient-based optimization, Nesterov acceleration, multiprocessor systems

BIOGRAPHY

Michael I. Jordan is the Pehong Chen Distinguished Professor in the Department of Electrical Engineering and Computer Science and the Department of Statistics at the University of California, Berkeley. He received his Masters in Mathematics from Arizona State University, and earned his PhD in Cognitive Science in 1985 from the University of California, San Diego. He was a professor at MIT from 1988 to 1998.

His research interests bridge the computational, statistical, cognitive and biological sciences, and have focused in recent years on Bayesian nonparametric analysis, probabilistic graphical models, spectral methods, kernel machines and applications to problems in distributed computing systems, natural language processing, signal processing and statistical genetics. Prof. Jordan is a member of the National Academy of Sciences, a member of the National Academy of Engineering and a member of the American Academy of Arts and Sciences. He is a Fellow of the American Association for the Advancement of Science. He has been named a Neyman Lecturer and a Medallion Lecturer by the Institute of Mathematical Statistics. He received the IJCAI Research Excellence Award in 2016, the David E. Rumelhart Prize in 2015 and the ACM/AAAI Allen Newell Award in 2009. He is a Fellow of the AAAI, ACM, ASA, CSS, IEEE, IMS, ISBA and SIAM.

SIGMETRICS'17, June 5-9, 2017, Urbana-Champaign, IL, USA.
ACM ISBN 978-1-4503-5032-7/17/06.
http://dx.doi.org/10.1145/3078505.3078506

Portfolio-driven Resource Management for Transient Cloud Servers[*]

Prateek Sharma
University of Massachusetts Amherst

David Irwin
University of Massachusetts Amherst

Prashant Shenoy
University of Massachusetts Amherst

1 INTRODUCTION

Cloud computing has become popular in recent years for a wide range of applications, including latency-sensitive web services, computationally-intensive scientific workloads, and data-intensive parallel tasks. Recently, cloud platforms have introduced a new class of servers, called *transient servers*, which they may unilaterally revoke at any time. Transient servers (such as Amazon EC2 spot instances and Google preemptible VMs) typically incur a fraction of the cost of their regular ("on-demand") server counterparts.

However, transient server revocations, which are akin to fail-stop failures, can lead to severe disruption in application performance and availability. Thus, despite the low cost of transient servers, making effective use of this new class of servers remains challenging. To minimize the effect of transient server revocations, applications must carefully select their fault-tolerance policy. Different applications, such as Spark, MapReduce, and MPI, have different tolerances to revocations, and require different application-specific mechanisms to handle revocations and their subsequent recovery. In addition, cloud providers provide a large number of transient servers with potentially different costs and failure-rates. For example, Amazon offers more than 250 spot instances in the US-East-1 region, and more than 2,500 globally. Thus in addition to fault tolerance policies, applications must also carefully select transient servers, if they seek to minimize their costs and running times.

2 SERVER PORTFOLIOS

To address the problem of transient server selection , we introduce a model-driven framework called *server portfolios*. Portfolios represent a virtual cloud cluster composed of a mix of transient server types with configurable cost and availability depending on the application's tolerance to revocation risk and price sensitivity (Figure 1). Our portfolio model derives from Modern Portfolio Theory in financial economics, which enables investors to methodically construct a financial portfolio from a large number of underlying assets with various risks and rewards.

The flexibility and explicit risk-awareness that portfolios offer is not provided by prior work on transient server selection, which focuses largely on selecting *one* server type (among the hundreds that cloud providers offer). In contrast, portfolios are a *general* technique for constructing *heterogeneous* collections of servers for a wide

[*]Full version of the paper available at http://lass.cs.umass.edu/publications/pdf/exosphere-sigmetrics17.pdf

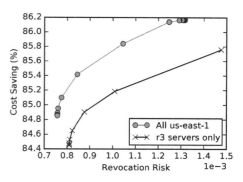

Figure 1: Given an application's risk averseness, server portfolios provide lowest-cost heterogenous virtual server clusters. Choosing a portfolio from a larger collection of servers (all US-east-1 vs. only r3) results in higher cost saving.

range of risk tolerances and application preferences. We use portfolio modeling as part of the design of an application-independent framework for supporting transiency, called ExoSphere. ExoSphere uses portfolio modeling to expose virtual clusters of transient servers of different types to different applications.

Along with portfolio modeling, ExoSphere also supports custom application-specific policies for handling transiency. In particular, ExoSphere adopts an Exokernel approach by exposing a set of basic mechanisms that are common to all transiency-enabled applications. These mechanisms can be used by applications to design custom policies for handling revocations, saving state, and performing recovery. We distill a general set of transiency-specific policies and mechanisms into a well-defined API that is exposed to applications. Applications then implement various policies in handler functions defined in the API, which are triggered based on changing market conditions, e.g., when prices increase or a revocation occurs.

3 EVALUATION

We have implemented ExoSphere by extending Mesos and integrating it with EC2's spot market. ExoSphere's transiency API allows us to develop transiency-aware variants of multiple applications such as Spark, MPI, and BOINC, with modest effort. ExoSphere simplifies the development of these applications, while also improving their performance and decreasing costs compared to prior approaches.

Compared to existing greedy approaches, ExoSphere's diversified portfolios can mitigate the risk of simultaneous revocations by more than 10×, while achieving more than 80% cost savings compared to on-demand servers.

Optimal Posted Prices for Online Cloud Resource Allocation[*]

Zijun Zhang
Dept. of Computer Science
University of Calgary
zijun.zhang@ucalgary.ca

Zongpeng Li
Dept. of Computer Science
University of Calgary
zongpeng@ucalgary.ca

Chuan Wu
Dept. of Computer Science
The University of Hongkong
cwu@cs.hku.hk

ABSTRACT

Cloud computing has proliferated as the new computing paradigm that provides flexible, on-demand computing services in a pay-as-you-go fashion. Given fixed cloud resource capacity, a fundamental problem is to determine which user demands to satisfy at each time point, for maximizing the social welfare of the cloud eco-system. Such cloud resource allocation in practice requires *online decision making* upon arrivals of job requests. A natural, *de facto* standard here is a *posted pricing mechanism*: the cloud provider publishes resource prices; cloud users act as price takers who accept/reject the cloud service by comparing the prices with their job valuations.

Major cloud providers today typically post fixed prices, while dynamic pricing based on realtime demand-supply could be an more efficient alternative [1]. Since the Spot Instances model in Amazon EC2, various dynamic pricing strategies have emerged, including auction mechanisms [6, 8, 9], and other dynamic pricing strategies for revenue maximization and efficient cloud resource utilization [4, 7].

This work studies effective pricing functions for a cloud provider to employ, for computing unit resource prices at each time point. Our study of the pricing functions has been partly inspired by dual price design in competitive online algorithms based on the classic primal-dual framework [2]. A key idea there is to update dual prices using exponential functions for making primal resource allocation decisions, leading to provable competitive ratios. Nonetheless, no explicit justifications were provided in the literature on the choice of using exponential dual price functions.

We first study the basic case of a single type of cloud resource without resource recycling, and design resource pricing functions based on the current resource utilization levels that capture realtime demand-supply of cloud resources. We prove the optimality of our pricing function design. We then investigate the cases of multiple resource types, and limited resource occupation durations. Our contributions include:

First, we justify the use of exponential pricing functions in the literature of both cloud computing [5, 8, 9] and online algorithms [2], both from a theoretical point of view and with intuitive interpretation. We prove the optimality of the exponential pricing function.

Second, we construct optimal pricing functions for more realistic cloud resource allocation scenarios, where the potential total demand of resources is bounded. Interestingly, this result also contributes to the literature on knapsack problems, in that our problem is closely related to a variant of the online knapsack problem [3, 10], where the total weight of items is upper bounded.

Third, we extend the pricing functions to take into account multiple resource types. We propose a joint pricing and scheduling strategy over multiple time slots. We further prove tight competitive ratios for these scenarios.

We further verify effectiveness of our price design in realistic cloud computing scenarios using simulation studies, relaxing assumptions made in the theoretical analysis. Finally, we note that our pricing models and algorithms are generally applicable to posted pricing mechanism design in other online resource allocation systems, which share similar characteristics as a cloud computing system.

KEYWORDS

Cloud Computing; Posted Pricing; Resource Allocation; Online Algorithms; Competitive Analysis

ACM Reference format:
Zijun Zhang, Zongpeng Li, and Chuan Wu. 2017. Optimal Posted Prices for Online Cloud Resource Allocation. In *Proceedings of SIGMETRICS '17, Urbana-Champaign, IL, USA, June 5–9, 2017,* 1 pages.
https://doi.org/http://dx.doi.org/10.1145/3078505.3078529

---

[*]The full version of the paper is available at https://arxiv.org/abs/1704.05511

REFERENCES

[1] May Al-Roomi, Shaikha Al-Ebrahim, Sabika Buqrais, and Imtiaz Ahmad. 2013. Cloud computing pricing models: a survey. *International Journal of Grid and Distributed Computing* 6, 5 (2013), 93–106.

[2] Niv Buchbinder and Joseph Naor. 2009. The design of competitive online algorithms via a primal: dual approach. *Foundations and Trends® in Theoretical Computer Science* 3, 2–3 (2009), 93–263.

[3] Deeparnab Chakrabarty, Yunhong Zhou, and Rajan Lukose. 2008. Online knapsack problems. In *Workshop on internet and network economics (WINE)*.

[4] Marian Mihailescu and Yong Meng Teo. 2010. Dynamic resource pricing on federated clouds. In *Proceedings of the 2010 10th IEEE/ACM International Conference on Cluster, Cloud and Grid Computing.* IEEE Computer Society, 513–517.

[5] Weijie Shi, Chuan Wu, and Zongpeng Li. 2016. An online mechanism for dynamic virtual cluster provisioning in geo-distributed clouds. In *Computer Communications, IEEE INFOCOM 2016-The 35th Annual IEEE International Conference on.* IEEE.

[6] Weijie Shi, Linquan Zhang, Chuan Wu, Zongpeng Li, and Francis Lau. 2014. An online auction framework for dynamic resource provisioning in cloud computing. *ACM SIGMETRICS Performance Evaluation Review* 42, 1 (2014), 71–83.

[7] Hong Xu and Baochun Li. 2013. Dynamic cloud pricing for revenue maximization. *IEEE Transactions on Cloud Computing* 1, 2 (2013), 158–171.

[8] Xiaoxi Zhang, Zhiyi Huang, Chuan Wu, Zongpeng Li, and Francis Lau. 2015. Online auctions in IaaS clouds: welfare and profit maximization with server costs. In *ACM SIGMETRICS Performance Evaluation Review,* Vol. 43. ACM, 3–15.

[9] Ruiting Zhou, Zongpeng Li, Chuan Wu, and Zhiyi Huang. 2016. An Efficient Cloud Market Mechanism for Computing Jobs With Soft Deadlines. *IEEE/ACM Transactions on Networking* (2016).

[10] Yunhong Zhou, Deeparnab Chakrabarty, and Rajan Lukose. 2008. Budget constrained bidding in keyword auctions and online knapsack problems. In *International Workshop on Internet and Network Economics.* Springer, 566–576.

On Optimal Two-Sided Pricing of Congested Networks

Xin Wang
University of Science and Technology of China
yixinxa@mail.ustc.edu.cn

Richard T. B. Ma
School of Computing, National University of Singapore
tbma@comp.nus.edu.sg

Yinlong Xu
University of Science and Technology of China
ylxu@ustc.edu.cn

ABSTRACT

Internet Access Providers (APs) have built massive network platforms by which end-users and Content Providers (CPs) can connect and transmit data to each other. Traditionally, APs adopt one-sided pricing schemes and obtain revenues mainly from end-users. With the fast development of data-intensive services, e.g., online video streaming and cloud-based applications, Internet traffic has been growing rapidly. To sustain the traffic growth and enhance user experiences, APs have to upgrade network infrastructures and expand capacities; however, they feel that the revenues from end-users are insufficient to recoup the corresponding costs. Consequently, some APs, e.g., Comcast and AT&T, have recently shifted towards two-sided pricing schemes, i.e., they start to impose termination fees on CPs' data traffic in addition to charging end-users.

Although some previous work has studied the economics of two-sided pricing in network markets, network congestion and its impacts on the utilities of different parties were often overlooked. However, the explosive traffic growth has caused severe congestion in many regional and global networks, especially during peak hours, which degrades end-users' experiences and reduces their data demand. This will strongly affect the profits of APs and the utilities of end-users and CPs. For optimizing individual and social utilities, APs and regulators need to reflect the design of pricing strategies and regulatory policies accordingly. So far, little is known about 1) the optimal two-sided pricing structure in a congested network and its changes under varying network environments, e.g., capacities of APs and congestion sensitivities of users, and 2) potential regulations on two-sided pricing for protecting social welfare from monopolistic providers. To address these questions, one challenge is to accurately capture endogenous congestion in networks. Although the level of congestion is influenced by network throughput, the users' traffic demand and throughput are also influenced by network congestion. It is crucial to capture this endogenous congestion so as to faithfully characterize the impacts of two-sided pricing in congested networks.

The full version of this paper, including models, theoretic analysis, and numerical simulations, is available at http://arxiv.org/abs/1704.03641.

The authors, X. Wang and Y. Xu, are also with AnHui Province Key Laboratory of High Performance Computing (USTC).

This work is supported in part by National Science Foundation of China (61379038), Huawei Innovation Research Program, Singapore MoE grant R-252-000-572-112, and National Research Foundation, Prime Minister's Office, Singapore under its Corporate Laboratory@University Scheme, National University of Singapore, and Singapore Telecommunications Ltd.

SIGMETRICS '17, June 5–9, 2017, Urbana-Champaign, IL, USA
ACM ISBN 978-1-4503-5032-7/17/06.
DOI: http://dx.doi.org/10.1145/3078505.3078588

In this work, we propose a novel model of a two-sided congested network built by an AP. We model network congestion as a function of AP's capacity and network throughput, which is also a function of the congestion level. We use different forms of the functions to capture congestion metric based on different service models, e.g., M/M/1 queue or capacity sharing, and user traffic based on different data types, e.g., online video or text. We characterize users' population and traffic demand under pricing and congestion parameters and derive an endogenous system congestion under an equilibrium. Based on the equilibrium model, we explore the structures of two-sided pricing which optimize the AP's profit and social welfare. We analyze the sensitivities of the optimal pricing under varying model parameters, .e.g., the capacity of the AP and congestion sensitivity of users. By comparing the two types of optimal pricing, we derive regulatory implications from the perspective of social welfare. Besides, we also evaluate the incentives of the AP and regulators to adopt the two-sided pricing instead of the traditional one-sided pricing that only charges on the user side.

The main results and implications of our work include the following. First, the structures of optimal pricing are related with an elasticity of system throughput, which reflects the effects of congestion on two-sided networks. Our result shows that to optimize the profits, APs should set two-sided prices to equalize the demand hazard rates on the user and CP sides, whose optimal value changes with the elasticity of throughput. However, to protect social welfare, the prices should be regulated such that the difference in the demand hazard rates of the two sides will enlarge as the elasticity of throughput decreases. Second, the changes of optimal pricing under varying AP's capacity and users' congestion sensitivity are largely driven by the type of data traffic. In particular, our result implies that when network traffic is mainly for online video, APs would increase two-sided prices under expanded capacity, while regulators may want to tighten the price regulation on the side of higher market power. However, when network traffic is mostly for text content, they should take the opposite operations. Third, as the capacities of APs and the demand for video traffic grow in the current Internet, APs and regulators will have increasing incentives to shift from the traditional one-sided pricing to the two-sided pricing because it will bring higher growth rates for both APs' profit and social welfare.

KEYWORDS

Two-sided pricing; network congestion; profit optimization; welfare optimization

ACM Reference format:
Xin Wang, Richard T. B. Ma, and Yinlong Xu. 2017. On Optimal Two-Sided Pricing of Congested Networks. In *Proceedings of SIGMETRICS '17, June 5–9, 2017, Urbana-Champaign, IL, USA, , 1 pages.*
DOI: http://dx.doi.org/10.1145/3078505.3078588

Matrix Factorization at the Frontier of Non-convex Optimizations

Abstract for SIGMETRICS 2017 Rising Star Award Talk

Sewoong Oh
University of Illinois, Urbana-Champaign

ABSTRACT

Principal Component Analysis (PCA) and Canonical Component Analysis (CCA) are two of the few examples of non-convex optimization problems that can be solved efficiently with sharp guarantees. This is achieved by the classical and well-established understanding of matrix factorizations. Recently, several new theoretical and algorithmic challenges have arisen in statistical learning over matrix factorizations, motivated by various real-world applications. Despite the inherent non-convex nature of these problem, efficient algorithms are being discovered with provable guarantees, extending the frontier of our understanding of non-convex optimization problems. I will present several recent results in this area in applications to matrix completion and sensing, crowdsourcing, ranking, and tensor factorization.

CCS CONCEPTS

• **Theory of computation** → **Design and analysis of algorithms**; *Mathematical Optimization*→ Continuous optimization; **Theory and algorithms for application domains**; *Mathematical Optimization*→ Machine learning theory

KEYWORDS

Matrix factorization; Principal Component Analysis; Non-convex optimization

BIOGRAPHY

Sewoong Oh is an Assistant Professor in the Department of Industrial and Enterprise Systems Engineering at UIUC. He received his PhD from the department of Electrical Engineering at Stanford University. Following his PhD, he worked as a postdoctoral researcher at Laboratory for Information and Decision Systems (LIDS) at MIT. He was co-awarded the Kenneth C. Sevcik outstanding student paper award at the SIGMETRICS 2010 and the best paper award at the SIGMETRICS 2015. He is a recipient of the NSF CAREER award and Google Faculty Research Award in 2016. His research interest includes matrix/tensor factorizations, graphical models, network analysis, and correlation analysis, with applications in social computing, computational biology, and privacy.

Outward Influence and Cascade Size Estimation in Billion-scale Networks

Hung T. Nguyen,
Tri P. Nguyen
Virginia Commonwealth Univ.
Richmond, VA 23220
{hungnt,trinpm}@vcu.edu

Tam N. Vu
Univ. of Colorado, Boulder &
UC Denver
Boulder, CO 80309
tam.vu@colorado.edu

Thang N. Dinh
Virginia Commonwealth Univ.
Richmond, VA 23220
tndinh@vcu.edu

ABSTRACT

In the past decade, a massive amount of data on human interactions has shed light on various cascading processes from the propagation of information and influence to the outbreak of diseases [3]. These cascading processes can be modeled in graph theory through the abstraction of the network as a graph $G = (V, E)$ and a *diffusion model* that describes how the cascade proceeds into the network from a prescribed subset of nodes. A fundamental task in analyzing those cascades is to estimate the cascade size, also known as *influence spread* in social networks. This task is the foundation of the solutions for many applications including viral marketing [3, 6], estimating users' influence [4], optimal vaccine allocation, identifying critical nodes in the network, and many others. Yet this task becomes computationally challenging in the face of the nowadays social networks that may consist of billions of nodes and edges.

Most existing work in network cascades uses stochastic diffusion models and estimates the influence spread through sampling [1, 3, 4]. The common practice is to use a fixed number of samples, e.g. 10K or 20K [1, 3], to estimate the expected size of the cascade, aka *influence spread*. Not only is there no single sample size that works well for all networks of different sizes and topologies, but those approaches also do not provide any accuracy guarantees. Recently, Lucier et al. [4] introduced INFEST, the first estimation method that comes with accuracy guarantees. Unfortunately, our experiments suggest that INFEST does not perform well in practice, taking hours on networks with only few thousand nodes. *Will there be a rigorous method to estimate the cascade size in billion-scale networks?*

Our contributions are summarized in the following.

- We introduce a new influence measure, called *Outward Influence* which is more effective in differentiating nodes' influence. We investigate the characteristics of this new measure including non-monotonicity, submodularity, and #P-hardness of computation.
- We propose two fully polynomial time randomized approximation schemes SIEA and SOIEA to provide (ϵ, δ)-approximate for influence spread and outward influence with only an $O(n)$ observed influence in total. Particularly, SOIEA, our algorithm to estimate influence spread,

is $\Omega(\log^4 n)$ *times faster* than the state-of-the-art INFEST [4] in theory and is *four to five orders of magnitude faster* than both INFEST and the naive Monte-Carlo sampling.

- A building block of SIEA is the robust mean estimation algorithm, termed RSA. This can be used to estimate influence spread under *other stochastic diffusion models*, or, in general, mean of bounded random variables of unknown distribution, extending the work of [2]. RSA will be our favorite statistical algorithm moving forwards.
- We perform comprehensive experiments on both real-world and synthesis networks with size up to 65 million nodes and *1.8 billion edges*. Our experiments indicate the superior of our algorithms in terms of both accuracy and running time in comparison to the naive Monte-Carlo and the state-of-the-art methods. The results also give *evidence against the practice of using a fixed number of samples* to estimate the cascade size. For example, using 10000 samples to estimate the influence will deviate up to 240% from the ground truth in a Twitter subnetwork. In contrast, our algorithm can provide (pseudo) *ground truth* with guaranteed small (relative) error (e.g. 0.5%). Thus it is a more concrete benchmark tool for research on network cascades.

The full paper is available at [5].

KEYWORDS

Outward Influence; Cascade Size Estimation; Billion-scale Networks

ACM Reference format:
Hung T. Nguyen, Tri P. Nguyen, Tam N. Vu, and Thang N. Dinh. 2017. Outward Influence and Cascade Size Estimation in Billion-scale Networks. In *Proceedings of SIGMETRICS '17, Urbana-Champaign, IL, USA, June 05-09, 2017*, 1 pages.
DOI: http://dx.doi.org/10.1145/3078505.3078526

REFERENCES

[1] E. Cohen, D. Delling, T. Pajor, and R. F. Werneck. 2014. Sketch-based influence maximization and computation: Scaling up with guarantees. In *CIKM*. ACM, 629–638.
[2] P. Dagum, R. Karp, M. Luby, and S. Ross. 2000. An Optimal Algorithm for Monte Carlo Estimation. *SICOMP* (2000), 1484–1496.
[3] D. Kempe, J. Kleinberg, and É. Tardos. 2003. Maximizing the spread of influence through a social network. In *KDD*. 137–146.
[4] B. Lucier, J. Oren, and Y. Singer. 2015. Influence at scale: Distributed computation of complex contagion in networks. In *KDD*. ACM, 735–744.
[5] H. T. Nguyen, Nguyen T. P., T. Vu, and T. N. Dinh. 2017. Outward Influence and Cascade Size Estimation in Billion-scale Networks. http://arxiv.org/abs/1704.04794.
[6] H. T. Nguyen, M. T. Thai, and T. N. Dinh. 2016. Stop-and-Stare: Optimal Sampling Algorithms for Viral Marketing in Billion-scale Networks. In *SIGMOD*. 695–710. https://arxiv.org/abs/1605.07990.

Accelerating Performance Inference over Closed Systems by Asymptotic Methods

Giuliano Casale
Imperial College London
London SW7 2AZ, UK
g.casale@imperial.ac.uk

ABSTRACT

Recent years have seen a rapid growth of interest in exploiting monitoring data collected from enterprise applications for automated management and performance analysis. In spite of this trend, even simple performance inference problems involving queueing theoretic formulas often incur computational bottlenecks, for example upon computing likelihoods in models of batch systems. Motivated by this issue, we revisit the solution of multiclass closed queueing networks, which are popular models used to describe batch and distributed applications with parallelism constraints. We first prove that the normalizing constant of the equilibrium state probabilities of a closed model can be reformulated exactly as a multidimensional integral over the unit simplex. This gives as a by-product novel explicit expressions for the multiclass normalizing constant. We then derive a method based on cubature rules to efficiently evaluate the proposed integral form in small and medium-sized models. For large models, we propose novel asymptotic expansions and Monte Carlo sampling methods to efficiently and accurately approximate normalizing constants and likelihoods. We illustrate the resulting accuracy gains in problems involving optimization-based inference.

ACM Reference format:
Giuliano Casale. 2017. Accelerating Performance Inference over Closed Systems by Asymptotic Methods. In *Proceedings of SIGMETRICS '17, June 5–9, 2017, Urbana-Champaign, IL, USA, ,* 1 pages.
DOI: http://dx.doi.org/10.1145/3078505.3078514

1 MODEL

We consider closed queueing networks with K single-server nodes, $M - K$ infinite server nodes, R job classes, and product-form solution [1]. Let N_r be the number of jobs in class r and let $N = (N_1, \ldots, N_R)$, $N = \sum_r N_r$. Let $\theta = [\theta_{kr}]$ collect the service demands placed by class-r jobs at node k. The model has state space $S_M = \{n \in \mathbb{N}^{MR} \mid n_{kr} \geq 0, \sum_{k=1}^{M} n_{kr} = N_r\}$, where n_{kr} is the number of class-r jobs at node k. The normalizing constant of the state probabilities is given by [1]

$$G_{\theta}(N) = \sum_{n \in S_M} \prod_{i=1}^{K} n_i! \prod_{k=1}^{M} \prod_{r=1}^{R} \frac{\theta_{kr}^{n_{kr}}}{n_{kr}!} \qquad (1)$$

We study how to efficiently obtain $G_{\theta}(N)$, motivated by the problem of computing likelihoods for model parameterization, model selection, and statistical inference.

2 MAIN RESULTS

For networks without infinite servers, we show in [2] that an exact integral form for the normalizing constant is given by

$$G_{\theta}(N) = \frac{(N + K - 1)!}{N_1! \cdots N_R!} \int_{\Delta_K} \prod_{r=1}^{R} \left(\sum_{k=1}^{K} \theta_{kr} u_k \right)^{N_r} du \qquad (2)$$

where $\Delta_K = \{u \in \mathbb{R}^K \mid u_i \geq 0, \sum_i u_i = 1\}$ is the unit simplex. Stemming from this novel integral form, [2] proposes exact and approximate computational methods for $G_{\theta}(N)$. For example, using cubature rules [3], (2) can be interpolated, either exactly or approximately, as

$$G_{\theta}(N) = \frac{(N + K - 1)!}{\prod_{s=1}^{R} N_s!} \sum_{i=0}^{S} w_i \sum_{\substack{b \geq 0: \\ b = S-i}} \prod_{r=1}^{R} \left(\sum_{j=1}^{K} \frac{(2b_j + 1)\theta_{jr}}{(2S + K - 2i)} \right)^{N_r} \qquad (3)$$

where S specifies the interpolation degree, $b \in \mathbb{N}^K$, $b = \sum_{i=1}^{K} b_i$, and $w_i = (-1)^i 2^{-2S}(2S + K - 2i)^{2S+1}/(i!(2S + K - i)!)$. Expression (3) requires in $O(S^K)$ time and $O(1)$ space as N grows, and can be computed exactly by setting $S = \lceil (N - 1)/2 \rceil$.

Further, following a logistic transformation of the integrand of (2), it is possible to apply Laplace's method and obtain a $O(N^{-1})$ asymptotic expansion for $G_{\theta}(N)$. This requires to solve a system of nonlinear equations, similar to the queue-length equations used in mean-value analysis. The derivation of the expansion also yields a Monte Carlo sampling method, which trades computational cost for accuracy in computing $G_{\theta}(N)$. The above results extend to networks with infinite server nodes.

A numerical validation in [2] shows that cubature rules are very effective on small models, whereas the proposed asymptotic expansion is the most effective method on large models. Monte Carlo sampling is found to improve state-of-the-art algorithms in the case of models with several classes.

REFERENCES
[1] F. Baskett, K. M. Chandy, R. R. Muntz, F. G. Palacios. Open, closed, and mixed networks of queues with different classes of customers. *JACM*, 22:248–260, 1975.
[2] G. Casale. Accelerating Performance Inference over Closed Systems by Asymptotic Methods. In *Proc. ACM Meas. Anal. Comput. Syst. (POMACS)* 1:1, June 2017. Preprint: https://spiral.imperial.ac.uk/handle/10044/1/43431. DOI: http://dx.doi.org/10.1145/3084445.
[3] A. Grundmann, H.M. Möller. Invariant integration formulas for the n-simplex by combinatorial methods. *SIAM J. on Numerical Analysis*, 15(2):282–290, 1978.

This research has been partially funded by the European Union's Horizon 2020 research and innovation programme (644869) and by a UK EPSRC grant (EP/L00738X/1).

Quality and Cost of Deterministic Network Calculus – Design and Evaluation of an Accurate and Fast Analysis

Steffen Bondorf, Paul Nikolaus, and Jens B. Schmitt

Distributed Computer Systems (DISCO) Lab, University of Kaiserslautern, Germany

{bondorf,nikolaus,jschmitt}@cs.uni-kl.de

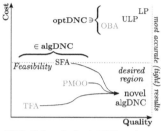

(a) Unifying algebraic DNC analyses.

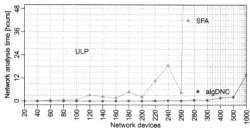

(b) Cost of analyses, measured in computation runtimes.

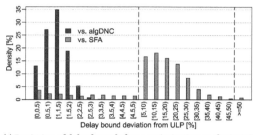

(c) Deviation of delay bounds from optimization analysis ULP.

Figure 1: Evaluation of quality and cost of deterministic network calculus analyses. Among algebraic (algDNC) and optimization (optDNC) analyses, only our novel algDNC achieves the desired tradeoff (a). For the networks feasible to analyze with optDNC's ULP analysis (b), our delay bounds only deviate by 1.142% on average; a decisive improvement over previous SFA (c).

ABSTRACT

Networks are integral parts of modern safety-critical systems and certification demands the provision of guarantees for data transmissions. Deterministic Network Calculus (DNC) can compute a worst-case bound on a data flow's end-to-end delay. Accuracy of DNC results has been improved steadily, resulting in two DNC branches: the classical algebraic analysis (algDNC) and the more recent optimization-based analysis (optDNC). The optimization-based branch provides a theoretical solution for tight bounds. Its computational cost grows, however, (possibly super-)exponentially with the network size. Consequently, a heuristic optimization formulation trading accuracy against computational costs was proposed. In this paper [1], we challenge optimization-based DNC with a novel algebraic DNC algorithm. We show that:

(1) no current optimization formulation scales well with the network size and

(2) algebraic DNC can be considerably improved in both aspects, accuracy and computational cost.

To that end, we contribute a novel DNC algorithm that transfers the optimization's search for best attainable delay bounds to algebraic DNC. It achieves a high degree of accuracy and our novel efficiency improvements reduce the cost of the analysis dramatically. In extensive numerical experiments, we observe that our delay bounds deviate from the optimization-based ones by only 1.142% on average while computation times simultaneously decrease by several orders of magnitude.

This work is supported by a Carl Zeiss Foundation grant.

Figure 1 presents the findings of our paper [1]: We combined the strengths of the algDNC analyses TFA, SFA, and PMOO to create a novel algDNC analysis that attains accurate delay bounds with feasible computational effort (Figure 1a). Against previous belief, we showed that optDNC's most efficient heuristic, ULP, is computationally infeasible even for moderately sized networks. For larger networks, we also showed that the algebraic SFA is more costly than expected, becoming barely feasible to execute. For our novel algDNC analysis, we provide efficiency improvements that make it scale considerably better with the network size, its computation times are several orders of magnitude smaller. (Figure 1b). Nonetheless, it provides highly accurate results that are crucially improving over SFA. Our algebraically derived delay bounds are competitive with optDNC's ULP (Figure 1c).

CCS CONCEPTS

• **Networks** → **Network performance evaluation**; *Network performance analysis*; Network performance modeling; • **Computing methodologies** → **Symbolic and algebraic algorithms**; *Symbolic calculus algorithms*; Optimization algorithms;

KEYWORDS

Delay bounds; deterministic network calculus; worst-case analysis

ACM Reference format:

Steffen Bondorf, Paul Nikolaus, and Jens B. Schmitt. 2017. Quality and Cost of Deterministic Network Calculus – Design and Evaluation of an Accurate and Fast Analysis . In *Proceedings of SIGMETRICS '17, June 5–9, 2017, Urbana-Champaign, IL, USA, , 1 pages.*

https://doi.org/http://dx.doi.org/10.1145/3078505.3078594

REFERENCES

[1] Steffen Bondorf, Paul Nikolaus, and Jens B. Schmitt. 2016. Quality and Cost of Deterministic Network Calculus – Design and Evaluation of an Accurate and Fast Analysis. *arXiv:1603.02094 [cs.NI]* (March 2016).

A Case Study in Power Substation Network Dynamics

David Formby
Georgia Institute of Technology
djformby@gatech.edu

Anwar Walid
Bell Laboratories
anwar.walid@alcatel-lucent.com

Raheem Beyah
Georgia Institute of Technology
rbeyah@ece.gatech.edu

ACM Reference format:
David Formby, Anwar Walid, and Raheem Beyah. 2017. A Case Study in Power Substation Network Dynamics. In *Proceedings of SIGMETRICS '17, June 5–9, 2017, Urbana-Champaign, IL, USA*, , 1 pages.
DOI: http://dx.doi.org/10.1145/3078505.3078525

1 INTRODUCTION

The modern world is becoming increasingly dependent on computing and communication technology to function, but unfortunately its application and impact on areas such as critical infrastructure and industrial control system (ICS) networks remains to be thoroughly studied. Significant research has been conducted to address the myriad security concerns in these areas, but they are virtually all based on artificial testbeds or simulations designed on assumptions about their behavior either from knowledge of traditional IT networking or from basic principles of ICS operation. In this work, we provide the most detailed characterization of an example ICS to date in order to determine if these common assumptions hold true. Although most predictions were found to be correct, some unexpected behavior was observed that highlights the fundamental differences between ICS and IT networks. The impact of these observations is discussed in terms of generality to other embedded networks, network security applications, and the suitability of the TCP protocol for this environment.

2 RESULTS

A live power distribution substation is observed over the course of two and a half years to measure its behavior and evolution over time. Then, a horizontal study is conducted that compared this behavior with three other substations from the same company. Observations were made on the datasets that offered new insight into round trip time estimation, TCP congestion control, and real-time operating system jitter in ICS networks.

Based on the low bandwidth usage and close geographic proximity, round trip times were initially predicted to be small and stable. However, Figure 1 illustrates how they are neither, and in fact depend primarily on the processing power and load of the embedded devices that make up the network.

This observation on round trip times was also found to be the likely cause behind relatively high and unbalanced retransmission rates, illustrated in Figure 2, and led to the conclusion that traditional TCP may not be well suited for embedded ICS environments.

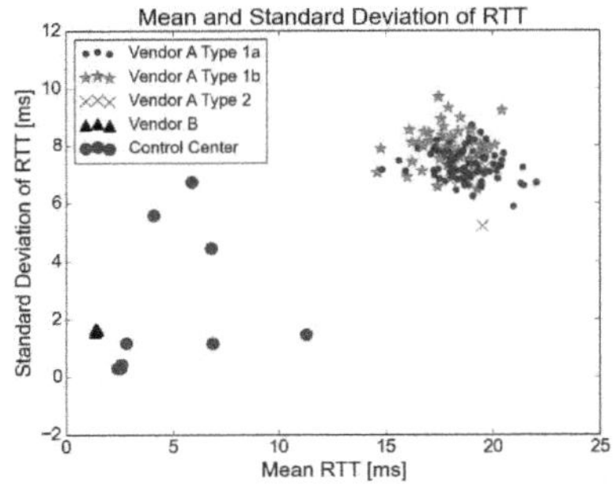

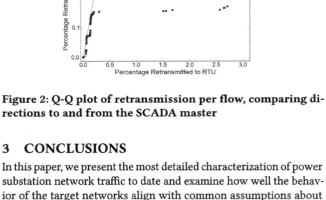

Figure 1: Mean and standard deviation of round trip times for each device

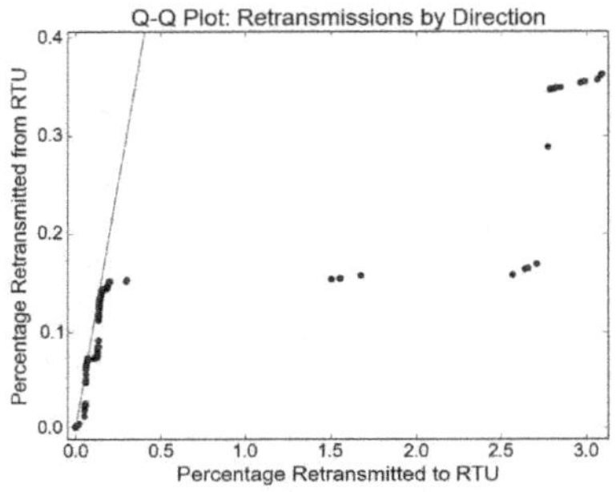

Figure 2: Q-Q plot of retransmission per flow, comparing directions to and from the SCADA master

3 CONCLUSIONS

In this paper, we present the most detailed characterization of power substation network traffic to date and examine how well the behavior of the target networks align with common assumptions about ICS and SCADA systems. We found that while most assumptions held true, there was also a surprising amount of unexpected behavior including slow and variable round trip times dominated by processing time, relatively high retransmission rates, and polling intervals with large jitter. Finally, evidence suggested that most of the various functions that TCP provides are largely irrelevant in the ICS environment. These observations are crucial to creating more accurate ICS network simulations and inspiring areas of new research. The full version of the paper may be found at http://cap.ece.gatech.edu/papers/sig17.pdf.

SIGMETRICS '17, June 5–9, 2017, Urbana-Champaign, IL, USA
 ACM ISBN 978-1-4503-5032-7/17/06.
DOI: http://dx.doi.org/10.1145/3078505.3078525

Persistent Spread Measurement for Big Network Data Based on Register Intersection*

You Zhou
Department of CISE
University of Florida, USA
youzhou@cise.ufl.edu

Yian Zhou
University of Florida
Google Inc., USA
yian@cise.ufl.edu

Min Chen
University of Florida
Google Inc., USA
min@cise.ufl.edu

Shigang Chen
Department of CISE
University of Florida, USA
sgchen@cise.ufl.edu

ABSTRACT

Persistent spread measurement is to count the number of distinct elements that persist in each network flow for pre-defined time periods. It has many practical applications, including detecting long-term stealthy network activities in the background of normal-user activities, such as stealthy DDoS attack, stealthy network scan, or faked network trend, which cannot be detected by traditional flow cardinality measurement. With big network data, one challenge is to measure the persistent spreads of a massive number of flows without incurring too much memory overhead as such measurement may be performed at the line speed by network processors with fast but small on-chip memory. We propose a highly compact Virtual Intersection HyperLogLog (VI-HLL) architecture for this purpose. It achieves far better memory efficiency than the best prior work of V-Bitmap, and in the meantime drastically extends the measurement range. Theoretical analysis and extensive experiments demonstrate that VI-HLL provides good measurement accuracy even in very tight memory space of less than 1 bit per flow.

CCS CONCEPTS

• **Networks → Network measurement**; **Network monitoring**; *Denial-of-service attacks*; *Network management*;

KEYWORDS

Persistent Spread Measurement; Big Network Data; Network Traffic Measurement; Network Security

*The full version of the paper is available at https://www.cise.ufl.edu/~sgchen/paper/sigmetrics17.pdf

ACM Reference format:
You Zhou, Yian Zhou, Min Chen, and Shigang Chen. 2017. Persistent Spread Measurement for Big Network Data Based on Register Intersection. In *Proceedings of SIGMETRICS '17, Urbana-Champaign, IL, USA, June 5–9, 2017*, 1 pages.
DOI: http://dx.doi.org/10.1145/3078505.3078593

Massive and distributed data are increasingly prevalent in modern networks as high-speed routers forward packets at hundreds of gigabits or even terabits per second. Big data also happens at the network edge. Traffic measurement and classification at such high speeds and with such massive volumes pose significant challenges.

Flow cardinality estimation is a fundamental problem in network traffic measurement. It estimates the number of *distinct* elements in every flow during pre-defined measurement periods. Each *flow* is uniquely identified by one or multiple fields in the packet headers, called *flow label*, which can be flexibly defined based on application needs. Existing research on flow cardinality estimation mainly focuses on analysing traffic sketches from one measurement period, which is the summary of the raw traffic data in that time period. This paper studies an under-investigated problem of analyzing sketches across multiple periods. In particular, we are interested in measuring the *persistent spread* of each flow, which is defined as the number of distinct elements that show up in a network flow during a certain number of consecutive measurement periods.

Our Contributions: First, we design a highly efficient persistent spread estimator called Intersection HLL (I-HLL) that works over multiple measurement periods. Second, to further improve memory efficiency, we introduce register sharing on top of I-HLL and propose a highly compact Virtual Intersection HLL (VI-HLL) architecture to measure the persistent spreads of a large number of flows simultaneously. Finally, the experimental results demonstrate the superior performance of VI-HLL.

ACKNOWLEDGMENTS

This work is supported in part by the National Science Foundation under grant STC-1562485 and a grant from Florida Center for Cybersecurity.

Deconstructing the Energy Consumption of the Mobile Page Load*

Yi Cao, Javad Nejati, Muhammad Wajahat, Aruna Balasubramanian, Anshul Gandhi

{yicao1,jnejati,mwajahat,arunab,anshul}@cs.stonybrook.edu

Stony Brook University

CCS CONCEPTS

• Networks → Network performance modeling; • Computing methodologies → Modeling methodologies;

KEYWORDS

Smartphones; Web Pages; Power Modeling

ACM Reference format:
Yi Cao, Javad Nejati, Muhammad Wajahat, Aruna Balasubramanian, Anshul Gandhi. 2017. Deconstructing the Energy Consumption of the Mobile Page Load. In *Proceedings of SIGMETRICS '17, Urbana-Champaign, IL, USA, June 5–9, 2017,* 1 pages.
https://doi.org/http://dx.doi.org/10.1145/3078505.3078587

1 BACKGROUND

Mobile Web page performance is critical to content providers, service providers, and users, as Web browsers are one of the most popular apps on phones. Slow Web pages are known to adversely affect profits and lead to user abandonment. While improving mobile web performance has drawn increasing attention, most optimizations tend to overlook an important factor, energy. Given the importance of battery life for mobile users, we argue that web page optimizations should be evaluated for their impact on energy consumption. However, examining the energy effects of a web optimization is challenging, even if one has access to power monitors, for several reasons. First, the page load process is relatively short-lived, ranging from several milliseconds to a few seconds. Fine-grained resource monitoring on such short timescales to model energy consumption is known to incur substantial overhead. Second, Web pages are complex. A Web enhancement can have widely varying effects on different page load activities. Thus, studying the energy impact of a Web enhancement on page loads requires understanding its effects on each page load activity. Existing approaches to analyzing mobile energy typically focus on profiling and modeling the resource consumption of the device during execution. Such approaches consider long-running services and apps such as games, audio, and video streaming, for which low-overhead, coarse-grained resource monitoring suffices. For page loads, however, coarse-grained resource

---

*The full version of the authors' paper is available at
https://www3.cs.stonybrook.edu/~yicao1/sigm17_paper16.pdf.

SIGMETRICS '17, June 5–9, 2017, Urbana-Champaign, IL, USA
© 2017 Copyright held by the owner/author(s).
ACM ISBN ACM ISBN 978-1-4503-5032-7/17/06
https://doi.org/http://dx.doi.org/10.1145/3078505.3078587

monitoring is not sufficient to analyze the energy consumption of individual, short-lived, page load activities.

2 OUR MODELING APPROACH – *RECON*

We present *RECON*(REsource- and COmpoNent-based modeling), a modeling approach that addresses the above challenges to estimate the energy consumption of any Web page load. The key intuition behind *RECON* is to go beyond resource-level information and *exploit application-level semantics* to capture the individual Web page load activities. Instead of modeling the energy consumption at the full page load level, which is too coarse grained, *RECON* models at a much finer *component* level granularity. Components are individual page load activities such as loading objects, parsing the page, or evaluating JavaScript.

To do this, *RECON* combines coarse-grained resource utilization and component-level Web page load information available from existing tools [1]. During the initial training stage, *RECON* uses a power monitor to measure the energy consumption during a set of page load processes and juxtaposes this power consumption with coarse-grained resource and component information. *RECON* uses both simple linear regression and more complex neural networks to build a model of the power consumption as a function of the resources used and the individual page load components, thus providing benefits over individual models. Using the model, *RECON* can estimate the energy consumption of any Web page loaded as-is or upon applying any enhancement, without the monitor.

3 RESULTS

We experimentally evaluate *RECON* on the Samsung Galaxy S4, S5, and Nexus devices using 80 Web pages. Comparisons with actual power measurements from a fine-grained power meter show that, using the linear regression model, *RECON* can estimate the energy consumption of the entire page load with a mean error of 6.3% and that of individual page load activity segments with a mean error of 16.4%. When trained as a neural network, *RECON*'s mean error for page energy estimation reduces to 5.4% and the mean segment error is 16.5%. We show that *RECON* can accurately estimate the energy consumption of a Web page under different network conditions, such as lower bandwidth or higher RTT, even when the model is trained under a default network condition. *RECON* also accurately estimates the energy consumption of a Web page after applying popular Web enhancements including ad blocking, inlining, compression, and caching.

REFERENCES

[1] Xiao Sophia Wang, Aruna Balasubramanian, Arvind Krishnamurthy, and David Wetherall. 2013. Demystifying Page Load Performance with WProf.. In *Proceedings of the 10th USENIX conference on Networked Systems Design and Implementation (NSDI '13)*. Lombard, IL, USA, 473–485.

Routing Money, Not Packets

A Tutorial on Internet Economics

Richard T. B. Ma
National University of Singapore
tbma@comp.nus.edu.sg

Vishal Misra
Columbia University
misra@cs.columbia.edu

ABSTRACT

This tutorial is in the broad area of Internet Economics, specifi-cally applying ideas from game theory, both Cooperative and Non-Cooperative. We consider the origins of the Internet architecture, and the evolution of the Internet ecosystem from a protocol and application standpoint. We next look at the evolution of the pricing structure on the Internet along three different dimensions: (a) be-tween ISPs, (b) between ISPs and content providers, and (c) between ISPs and end users. We present mathematical models describing the pricing structures in each dimension, the interaction between the three and competition amongst the entities leading to the notion of Network Neutrality. We look at various definitons of Network Neutrality and analyze the the impact of mechanisms like paid peer-ing, zero rating and differential pricing on the principle of Network Neutrality.

CCS CONCEPTS

•**Networks** →**Public Internet**; *Network performance modeling; Network performance analysis;*

KEYWORDS

Network Economics, Net Neutrality, Internet Governance, Premium Peering, Paid Prioritization, Shapley Value

ACM Reference format:
Richard T. B. Ma and Vishal Misra. 2017. Routing Money, Not Packets. In *Proceedings of SIGMETRICS '17, June 5–9, 2017, Urbana-Champaign, IL, USA, , 2 pages.*
DOI: http://dx.doi.org/10.1145/3078505.3083764

1 INTRODUCTION

The Internet has been and is still changing unexpectedly in many aspects. Started with elastic traffic and applications, e.g., emails and file downloading, we have seen significant rise in inelastic traffic, e.g., video and interactive web traffic, across the Internet. From a network perspective, the Internet originated from government-owned backbone networks, i.e., the ARPANET, and then evolved to a network of commercial Autonomous Systems (ASes) and Internet Service Providers (ISPs). Meanwhile, ISPs formed a hierarchical structure and were classified by tiers, with higher tier ISPs cover larger geographic regions and provide transit service for lower tier ISPs. However, large content providers, e.g., Google, are deploying

their own wide-area networks so as to bring content closer to users and bypassing Tier-1 ISPs on many paths, which is known as the *flattening phenomenon* of the Internet topology.

Changes in the content or network topology do not happen inde-pendently. Rather, they are driven by economics and the business relationships among the players in the Internet ecosystem. Not surprisingly, we have observed dramatic changes in the business re-lationships between the content providers and the ISPs and among the ISPs themselves. Traditionally, ISP settlements were often done bilaterally under either a (zero-dollar) peering or in the form of a customer-provider relationship. Tier-1 ISPs, e.g., Level 3, often charge lower tier ISPs for transit services and connect with each other under settlement-free peering. However, the Tier-1 ISPs do not have any guarantee in their profitability as the Internet evolves. For instance, we have seen exponential decrease (around 20% a year) in IP transit prices. Also, peering disputes happened, e.g., the de-peering between Cogent and Level 3 in 2005, where the lower tier ISPs that are closer to content or users refused to pay for the transit charge. This leads to the recent debate of network neutrality [1, 15], which reflects the ISPs' willingness to provide value-added and differentiated services [12, 16] and potentially charge content providers based on different levels of service quality.

The situation is further complicated by the emergence of new players in the ecosystem: Content Delivery Networks (CDNs), e.g., Akamai and Limelight, and high-quality video streaming providers, e.g., Netflix. From content providers' perspective, CDNs can deliver their content faster and more efficiently; from local ISPs' perspec-tive, CDNs can reduce the traffic volume from upstream, saving transit costs from their providers. Very often, ISPs do not charge the CDNs for putting servers in their networks. When the video stream-ing giant Netflix moved online a few years ago, its traffic surged immediately. Now it accounts for up to 32.7% of peak U.S. down-stream traffic and its traffic volume is higher than that of BitTorrent applications. Netflix used Limelight, one of the biggest CDNs, for content delivery, and later, the Tier-1 Level 3 also obtained a con-tract to deliver Netflix's traffic. Since most of the Netflix customers are based in the U.S., they often use Comcast, the biggest access ISP, as the last-mile access provider. Interestingly, Comcast managed to enter a so-called paid-peering relationship [2] with Level 3 and Limelight, under which the Tier-1 ISP and the CDN have to pay the access ISP for higher bandwidth on the last mile connection. This totally *reversed* the nominal customer-provider relationship where the Tier-1 ISP was the service provider and should have received payment for connectivity. Subsequently, Netflix entered into similar private peering arrangements with 4 major broadband ISPs in the US, where all those 4 major ISPs are de facto regional monopolies. Recently, the mobile operator T-Mobile recently of-fered a service called Binge On, where customers were not charged for bandwidth usage from major streaming providers like Netflix,

HBO etc. making them more attractive for users. In contrast to the wired broadband case T-Mobile *did not* charge the streaming providers anything for this service. This kind of differential pricing for content on the Internet, a mechanism called "zero rating" is another recent phenomena and is attracting a lot of controversy and regulatory intervention in places like India and Canada.

It is important to understand how these changes come about and what the driving factors are behind these changes, so as to get a sense of the desirable policies regulators might want to impose. In this tutorial, we discuss Internet economics problems in various aspects, including the impact of net neutrality policies, the strategic routing, peering and pricing decisions of ISPs and their interactions with content providers and end-users. We will use modeling and analytical approaches borrowed from economics, e.g., non-cooperative and coalition game theory, perform evaluation, e.g., queueing models to characterize network quality metrics such as throughput and delay. In particular, we will introduce a new equilibrium concept, *congestion equilibrium*, which naturally models the equilibrium state of a congested network under strategic interactions among the various stake holders, and a new policy alternative, called *Public Option*, for net neutrality.

2 OUTLINE

(1) The Internet Ecosystem and Evolution (15 mins)
- Macroscopic Internet evolution
  - The characteristics of traffic and applications
  - The flattening of the Internet topology
- Internet peering and peering disputes
  - Depeering between Level and Cogent
  - Peering dispute between Netflix and Comcast
- Internet governance and the net neutrality debate
  - Comcast vs. the U.S. FCC
  - The open Internet legislation

(2) Primer on Economics and Game Theory (15 mins)
- Congestion equilibrium [8]
- Non-cooperative and cooperative game theory

(3) The Shapley value and ISP settlement [6, 7, 11] (40 mins)
============= Tutorial Break [20 mins] =============

(4) Content-Side Pricing and Service Differentiation (40 mins)
- Public Option and Net Neutrality [9, 10, 13]
- Premium Peering [5]
- Sponsored Data and Subsidization Competition [3]

(5) Access-Side Pricing and Service Differentiation (30 mins)
- Data Cap and Usage-based Pricing [4]
- Optimal Service Differentiation [16]

(6) Optimal Two-Sided Pricing [14] (10 mins)

3 INTENDED AUDIENCE

This tutorial will be useful to policy makers, network researchers, engineers, and graduate students. It is aimed primarily at someone looking for understanding the fundamental driving forces of the Internet evolution, the Internet governance and policy issues, and the strategic interactions among the different stake-holders, i.e., content/application providers, ISPs and end-users. Background knowledge about one or more of the following topics is desirable:

(1) Basic economics concepts
(2) Game theory
(3) Network protocol and architecture
(4) Performance model and analysis

REFERENCES

[1] Nicholas Economides and Joacim Tag. 2012. Network Neutrality and Network Management Regulation: Quality of Service, Price Discrimination, and Exclusive Contracts. *Research Handbook on Governance of the Internet. Ed. Ian Brown. London: Edward Elgar* (2012).
[2] P. Faratin, D. Clark, P. Gilmore, S. Bauer, A. Berger, and W. Lehr. 2007. Complexity of Internet Interconnections: Technology, Incentives and Implications for Policy. *The 35th Research Conference on Communication, Information and Internet Policy (TPRC)* (2007).
[3] Richard T. B. Ma. 2016. Subsidization Competition: Vitalizing the Neutral Internet. *IEEE/ACM Transactions on Networking* 24, 4 (2016).
[4] Richard T. B. Ma. 2016. Usage-Based Pricing and Competition in Congestible Network Service Markets. *IEEE/ACM Transactions on Networking* 24, 5 (2016).
[5] Richard T. B. Ma. 2017. Pay or Perish: The Economics of Premium Peering. *IEEE Journal on Selected Areas of Communications* 35, 2 (February 2017).
[6] Richard T. B. Ma, Dahming Chiu, John C.S. Lui, Vishal Misra, and Dan Rubenstein. 2010. Internet Economics: The use of Shapley value for ISP settlement. *IEEE/ACM Transactions on Networking* 18, 3 (June 2010).
[7] Richard T. B. Ma, Dahming Chiu, John C.S. Lui, Vishal Misra, and Dan Rubenstein. 2011. On Cooperative Settlement Between Content, Transit and Eyeball Internet Service Providers. *IEEE/ACM Transactions on Networking* 19, 3 (2011).
[8] Richard T. B. Ma and Vishal Misra. 2012. Congestion and Its Role in Network Equilibrium. *IEEE Journal on Selected Areas in Communications* 30, 11 (December 2012).
[9] Richard T. B. Ma and Vishal Misra. 2013. The Public Option: a Non-regulatory Alternative to Network Neutrality. *IEEE/ACM Transactions on Networking* 21, 6 (2013).
[10] Richard T. B. Ma, Jingjing Wang, and Dah Ming Chiu. 2017. Paid Prioritization and Its Impact on Net Neutrality. *IEEE Journal on Selected Areas of Communications* 35, 2 (February 2017).
[11] Vishal Misra. 2015. Routing Money, Not Packets. *Commun. ACM* 58, 6 (June 2015), 24–27.
[12] Nikhil Shetty, Galina Schwartz, and Jean Walrand. 2010. Internet QoS and Regulations. *IEEE/ACM Transactions on Networking* 18, 6 (December 2010).
[13] Jing Tang and Richard T. B. Ma. 2014. Regulating Monopolistic ISPs Without Neutrality. In *Proceedings of the 22nd IEEE International Conference on Network Protocols (ICNP)*. Raleigh, NC, USA.
[14] Xin Wang, Richard T. B. Ma, and Yinlong Xu. 2017. On Optimal Two-Sided Pricing of Congested Networks. In *Proceedings of the ACM Sigmetrics Conference, Champaign-Urbana, USA, June 5-9*.
[15] Tim Wu. 2005. Network Neutrality, Broadband Discrimination. *Journal of Telecommunications and High Technology Law* 141 (2005).
[16] Mao Zou, Richard T. B. Ma, Xin Wang, and Yinlong Xu. 2017. On Optimal Service Differentiation in Congested Network Markets. In *Proceedings of the IEEE International Conference on Computer Communications (INFOCOM), May 1st - 4th, Atlanta, GA, USA*.

Author Index